July 2022

Dear _____,

Just want to thank you for believing in The Calling and I and helping people around the world live out their God given dreams, knowing time is short and we are meant to live fearlessly after Jesus for such a time as this! Excited for all the ways we can dream together with The Chosen & The Calling! Thank You again for your belief in T.C. & I, it has changed our lives! The Best is yet to come, in Jesus!

Passion, Chrysandra

TO ALL THE DREAMERS

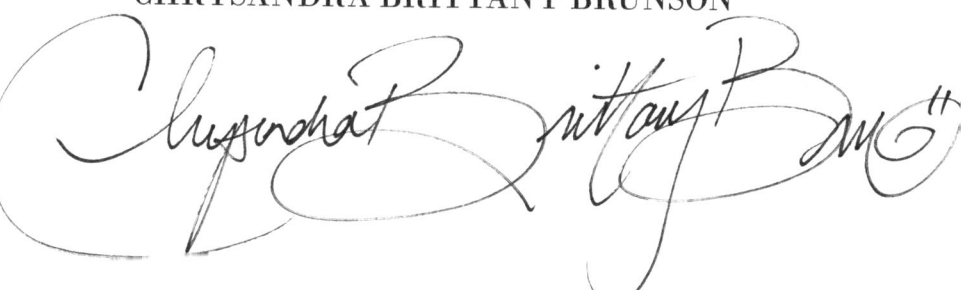

Keep Dreaming BIG!

CHRYSANDRA BRITTANY BRUNSON

WESTBOW PRESS
A DIVISION OF THOMAS NELSON
& ZONDERVAN

Copyright © 2021 Chrysandra Brittany Brunson.

All rights reserved. No part of this book may be used or reproduced by any means, graphic, electronic, or mechanical, including photocopying, recording, taping or by any information storage retrieval system without the written permission of the author except in the case of brief quotations embodied in critical articles and reviews.

This book is a work of non-fiction. Unless otherwise noted, the author and the publisher make no explicit guarantees as to the accuracy of the information contained in this book and in some cases, names of people and places have been altered to protect their privacy.

WestBow Press books may be ordered through booksellers or by contacting:

WestBow Press
A Division of Thomas Nelson & Zondervan
1663 Liberty Drive
Bloomington, IN 47403
www.westbowpress.com
844-714-3454

Because of the dynamic nature of the Internet, any web addresses or links contained in this book may have changed since publication and may no longer be valid. The views expressed in this work are solely those of the author and do not necessarily reflect the views of the publisher, and the publisher hereby disclaims any responsibility for them.

Any people depicted in stock imagery provided by Getty Images are models, and such images are being used for illustrative purposes only.
Certain stock imagery © Getty Images.

Scripture quotations are from the ESV® Bible (The Holy Bible, English Standard Version®), copyright © 2001 by Crossway, a publishing ministry of Good News Publishers. Used by permission. All rights reserved.

ISBN: 978-1-6642-4945-5 (sc)
ISBN: 978-1-6642-4947-9 (hc)
ISBN: 978-1-6642-4946-2 (e)

Library of Congress Control Number: 2021923041

Print information available on the last page.

WestBow Press rev. date: 11/15/2021

DEDICATION

This book is dedicated to the dreamer within each of our hearts, my dearest family, friends and especially Jesus Christ and His wild, wondrous and glorious love and imagination. Jesus, we ask you to do more than we could ever imagine so as to activate our callings in and throughout this book.

"We are each born to live out God's imagination."

Dedicated also in loving memory of all those experiencing Heaven right now and cheering us on, especially my Nana & Papa Barnett, Grandma & Grandpa Brunson, Uncle Scott Fredrickson, Michael Monard, Ray Ostlie, Bill Armstrong and all those who have gone before us and will forever be in our hearts. We love you and hope to make you proud living out your incredible legacy!

A very special thanks to every person who has supported The Calling to help people everywhere go after their God-given dreams!

A very special thank you to the
Brunson Family, Hauenstein Family, Barnett Family,
Young Family, Jordan Family, Bradshaw Family,
Evans Family, Harris Family, Fredrickson Family, Grenz Family,
Ellingsworth Family, Muchnik Family, Gonzalez Family,
Cottrell Family, Biggers Family, Ames Family, Travis Family,
Crain Family, Colter Family, Martin Family, Smith Family, Janssen
Family, Hamilton Family, Wiebe Family, Lohman Family, Crain
Family, Day Family, Ewen Family, McCormick Family, Dysick
Family, Wall Family, Sani Family, Eckenhoff Family, Omero Family,
Rothenfeld Family, Wilson Family, Henkelman Family, Ruis Family,
Jackson Family, Pettit Family, Sherrod Family, Baker Family, Haynes
Family, Brozovich Family, Tracey Family, Hanna Family, Imer Family,
Mains Family, Daniel Family, Bodly Family, Doll Family, Wheaton
Family, Allbaugh Family, Tally Family, Cox Family, Armstrong Family,
Andrews Family, Werner Family, Ruiz Family, Brown Family, Marc
Family, Porentas Family, McHugh Family, Dunn Family, Barrington
Family, Bragg Family, Hyatt Family, Costner Family, Sobolik Family,
Vogt Family, Medina Family, Monfort Family, Warren Family, Otteman
Family, DeLehman Family, Carrado Family, and so many others!

THIS BOOK IS WRITTEN FOR

This book is for all the Dreamers of the world. This book is for those who wholeheartedly believe that the future belongs to those who dream and yearn to live out God's calling for our lives. Each of us has been given a unique role to fulfill kingdom history for such a time as this. It is now your responsibility to pick the torch you have been given and the relight the flame of your dream once again. Do not let fear hold you back no matter your age, background of culture history. Now is your time and this book was made to let your soar into God's Imagination for you. Be inspired by Chrysandra Brunson's story of starting The Calling to ignite your true calling.

The question is, *'What would do if you knew you could not fail?'*

Other Tools from The Calling:
The Activation *Dream Kit*
Activation Sheet
All Calling Products
All Resources will be found on The Calling's website:
www.thecallingnonproft.org

ABOUT THE CALLING

The singular basis for all activities and goals associated with The Calling is the Gospel of Jesus Christ. This is our recognition that we are actively and naturally inclined to disobey God and the way of life he has prescribed for us. But God, with immense love for us, sent his son Jesus to receive the consequences of our rebellion. If we recognize our need for restoration, we simply need to trust God and trust that Christ's payment was enough. We will again find acceptance with God and therefore are made able to have an active relationship with him, in which he continues to love us at the depths of who we are with immense strength.

Our response of love to God comes in a very simple form: we obey. First of all, we obey his commandments and his command to love the people around us. Secondly, we obey the direction he gives us in our individual lives. Often, this can be the most difficult area to obey God because it is different for everyone. It is easy to be afraid of being wrong about what we hear him calling us to do. It is frightening to risk what we have in the present for an unsure future and it is difficult to trust God when we don't have a lot of evidence.

The Calling is not merely about making peoples' dreams come true – but about helping people understand and achieve the dreams God has given each individual. We trust that God is actively making the world what it needs to be and our role in that process is merely doing what he has asked us to do at an individual level. Your calling from God will never contradict the Gospel of Jesus Christ, the commands God has given us, including his commands to love him and others. We want to help you answer the questions:

1. What is God calling me to? 2. How do I fearlessly obey?

We are here to help you discern what God is calling you to and to encourage you to fearlessly obey. If it is a God calling, he will fulfill what He has promised!

Romans 3:23, John 3:16, John 14:15, Romans 8:28, 2 Peter 1:3-10

THE CALLING MISSION & VISION

The Calling is a non-profit 501(c)(3) headquartered in Denver, CO. The Calling exists to create a world where people live out their God-given calling, using their gifts to empower the lives of others.

The Calling creates global, custom programs to help individuals of all races, ages and gifts unleash and live out their God-given dreams, by empowering generational spiritual transformation in them to make a positive impact on culture across the world.

Specifically, The Calling inspires people to discover their gifts and talents, empowers people by connecting them to strategic partners and equips people by providing tools and resources to fulfill their calling.

In short, The Calling supports and equips people to achieve their calling and is committed to partnering with our dreamers on their journey.

ABOUT THE AUTHOR

Chrysandra Brittany Brunson, MBA, is one of America's most influential millennial female leaders, being the founder of the world-renowned non-profit, The Calling, headquartered in Denver, Colorado. She also holds a Master's Degree in Business Administration (MBA) from Colorado Christian University. Chrysandra has been invited to share The Calling with Former US Presidents, Congressman, Grammy award entertainment, fortune 100 companies, many Archdiocese's, professional athletic teams, Hollywood celebrities and most importantly, the poorest of the poor. She is on the National Faith Advisory Board, Chaplain of the NFL Denver Bronco Cheerleaders, Former CCU Alumni Council President, a Former Pro Mermaid, Former Miss Colorado's Choice for Miss Colorado Miss America and much more – giving her the perfect background to talk about living out God's big dreams for our lives!

This book shares the inside details of her life and how she started The Calling. Knowing that if she was able to go after her God-given calling, so could anyone else. Chrysandra started The Calling when she was only 18 years of age in 2007 at a public high school. Since then, it has grown to touch nations around the globe. The Calling has the vision to unleash people's true God-given calling by cultivating environments of ultimate inspiration. Providing activation tools, connections and educational training for people to live out their truest potential that reflects Heaven on Earth like never before.

Belief and courage are the key ingredients The Calling uses to tap into one's true potential and dreams. Chrysandra has led The Calling to produce historic events at Red Rocks Amphitheater, Civic Center Park, Haiti and has seen The Calling touching hearts around the world. She knows that God is the God of the seemingly impossible and that if He puts a dream in one's heart, no one can stop it except ourselves. Chrysandra knows that it is time to release the true potential of every heart to live out their God-given destiny. Chrysandra lives in Denver, Colorado, near her family and is always a flight away to spark the dreams of nations. Here's to all the Dreamers!

CONTENTS

Dedication v
About the Author xv
The Beginning 1
Chapter 1   To Be Written In History 3
Chapter 2   Work to Do in Heaven 14
Chapter 3   Living Out Your Calling 21
Chapter 4   How to Turn Your Dreams into Reality 44
Chapter 5   The Superhero Power of Courage 62
Chapter 6   Don't Let Obstacles Stop Your Dreams 87
Chapter 7   Walk Through The Impossible 104
Chapter 8   Romantic Relationships 113
Chapter 9   The Magic of Making The Most Of Every Situation 127
Chapter 10   Activation Sheet 133
Chapter 11   Calling Boot Camp 141
Conclusion 157

THE BEGINNING

The Beginning

One charming summer evening before my senior year of high school, my mom, sister and I took our annual trip to Southern California. As we drove around we stopped at the famous Crystal Cathedral in Orange County.

The church was a sacred place for my family. Almost every Sunday, my Papa and Nana used to watch a show called *Hour of Power*. The host, Robert A. Schuller, was an evangelist preaching at the church. Robert was an an ordained pastor having followed in his parent's footsteps.

On this night, there were no stirring sermons to consume, as the church was unfortunately closed. So we walked around, taking in all the sights. That's when we came across a little duckling stuck inside the building. The duckling's family was trying to get their tiny baby out of the building by pecking at the massive glass door it was caged behind.

We knew we needed to get help for the duckling, so we searched for a security guard who could help us. We finally found a guard right by the bronze statue of Jesus. The statue of Jesus was ushering Peter to walk on the water and trust Him to do the impossible. Was this a coincidence? I think not!

The security guard opened the door promptly and let the duckling out of the building to reunite with his family. Lucky for us, the guard then insisted that our family get a private tour of the famous church campus. If there is anything that one could learn from this is that nothing is ever a coincidence.

Taking the tour reminded me of all the work that Schuller had accomplished and how the church had become so much more than a building for millions of TV viewers. While his work at the church influenced a generation of worshippers, Robert gained wider acclaim for his sermons that were broadcasted.

By reaching an audience that extended far beyond the pews in front of him, Robert amplified his messages of faith all over the world. Though he shared many words of wisdom with his audience, there was one phrase in particular that truly stuck with people. It was the same quote I saw displayed prominently inside the cathedral when my family and I got our private tour: "What would you do if you knew you could not fail?"

That message bombarded my senses and made me rethink my entire existence. Robert Schuller's message stressed the importance of absolute, unshakable faith. If you believe in God, fully and completely, your faith can allow you to accomplish anything. Believe in God, believe in yourself and miracles can happen!

I was instantly motivated by this message! I realized that it would be the best way to motivate other people to learn to do exactly what God is calling them to do. My heart was ignited with a passion like never before – one that completely changed my life. *What would you do if you knew you could not fail?* This question became the guiding light for both my own spiritual journey and the journey that I hope to one day bring to millions. It would become the cornerstone of a movement that I would start - The Calling.

The mission of The Calling is to inspire and empower people to follow their dreams. It's to inspire others to find their purpose both in Heaven and Earth. If you truly have faith, if you believe in your heart of hearts that you cannot fail, then you can achieve anything. We are all meant to live out our calling.

My own journey accelerated that night at the church. That experience would set the stage for a surreal moment a few months later – one defined by my quest to help people of all backgrounds use faith to find their true calling.

This is that story—both mine and yours.

CHAPTER 1

To Be Written In History

To Be Written in History

The way to get started is to quit talking and begin doing.
—Walt Disney

What does it mean to be a history maker? I realize the term *history maker* may sound a little dramatic when you think of it as it relates to your life, but to think that is to minimize the possibilities that God wants to accomplish through you. I argue that we all have the opportunity to be history makers. Yes, to be people who influence 'HIStory' as only God destined us to do!

Most people shy away from the sight of a new idea because they are afraid of change. They're so used to living in their comfortable version of reality that they label anything that reeks the slightest of unfamiliarity as impractical. However, many historically infamous entrepreneurs, revolutionary figures and world leaders are those who had the courage and a willingness to challenge conventional wisdom. They are widely known today because they stood up for what they believed in at the cost of being singled out and ridiculed.

Centuries ago, when slavery started to spread like a plague in America, those comfortably seated in positions of power made it extremely dangerous for anyone to challenge the system. Nonetheless, Harriet Tubman rose to that challenge and made nineteen separate missions in a ten-year span to rescue over three hundred people from the shackles of slavery.

This was a woman who was born into slavery. She did not have mother or father that led an example of being such an activist. She possessed an inner courage to fight for a purpose that was close to God's heart, knowing that her life was going to be extremely endangered. Because she followed God's whisper, she is now known as a history maker. God has a purpose for each one of us to live out if we are willing to listen and act. When we do this, we each are able to have a chance for our courage to ripple out and change the story. In the Bible, God talks about the stories that will be written about us in Heaven and this is the true history book. The question is, 'What story will be written about you?' Now is the time to acknowledge God's calling on your life. You may have felt God's leading before and ignored it, but now is your time to believe in it and walk by faith, as you now know you will be written in history. You will become the beloved dreamer He has destined you to be.

MY HISTORY MOMENT

My role as a history maker started in high school.

For a moment, the world around me stood still. Yes, in the middle of a 5A high school passing period, which on any other day would compare to a modern-day human zoo, I had a God moment. It was in that moment God silenced my space. It wouldn't have mattered if the class clown were to trip someone right in front of me or if the whole cheerleading squad started a victory chant in the hallway; everything went silent. It was a moment between God and me alone. I know this story may seem unreal, but it was not; it was miraculous! God was speaking extraordinary things to an ordinary girl and paving the way for her future. If that hallway hadn't been lined with lockers, it could have been the Red Sea!

The vision God revealed to me there was intense! God spoke my God-given calling at the speed of light. In that moment, I felt it, heard it and because of that, in a sense it was like I experienced my future. From then on I have never looked back from pursuing it!

I learned you don't have to be in a church service to experience the miraculous! I found out that my purpose was to inspire people around the globe into their fullest God-given dream. I realized if you trust God for your dreams, as you move forward in it, your dream will be lived out and inspire others along the way to fulfill theirs!

THE DAY I FOUND THE VOICE OF GOD AND THUS MY TRUE CALLING

My future was being shaped as I was a senior at Bear Creek High School, varsity cheerleading captain, student body president, and a student in a class called Senior Project with Mr. Portentas. It was a class that allowed you to create any project you wanted and then write a paper on it. I knew I just had to join because at that point in my life I wanted to leave a lifelong legacy. This class was the perfect stepping-stone to do so. It took a while to discover what I wanted to do.

Many of my classmates knew exactly what their projects would be. They were confidently creating their projects and doing things like taking swing dance lessons, writing a cookbook and even building a snowboard. However, I had no idea what I was supposed to do, I was stuck, until that monumental moment occurred on an ordinary day. It was in that chaotic high school hallway when God reminded me of the quote He'd shown me the summer before. In that moment I was miraculously stopped. I heard the Lord say, "Chrysandra, so many of My children are afraid to go after the things I am calling them to and there is no reason to be afraid. I am right here with you, leading you all the way!" I heard all of it while standing still in the middle of a loud hallway with other students.

The voice echoed in my head over and over again until these words were imprinted onto my heart. The imprinting led me to wonder about all the possibilities that could happen if the people of God fearlessly embraced His calling on their lives. My imagination was immediately flooded with ideas of how to get the message out through conversations, workshops, businesses and even through global conferences, allowing communities and nations to come together and activate their calling all together.

This is when the vision of The Calling began for me. God showed my heart that so many people are afraid to live out their calling. He wanted to release the world into their fullest potential through this simple yet life-changing message and through all these different avenues. This message would be offered to souls all around the world to realize their fullest God-given potential, this includes YOU!

What I thought was a day like any other turned into one of the most extraordinary days of my life. I knew in my soul that this was what I had been born to do! The gift of The Calling has molded me into the person I am today.

God has a purpose for each one of us! A plan for us to live, where we can influence the people and world around us. God wants to be involved in all the details of our lives. When we know who our God is and who we are in Christ, our true calling is realized.

Paul writes in Ephesians 4:1 (ESV), "As a prisoner of the Lord then I urge you to live a life worthy of the calling you have received!"

This is a great opportunity and it is a choice. Many people know exactly what their calling is but do not act upon it. Those that view it as the best opportunity available to them, will never regret the legacy that they will leave.

God revealed to me the power that can come from people gathering together to be inspired by speakers, bands, businesses and organizations as we are all unified and inspired. The goal of The Calling is for individuals to walk away ready to take action in realizing their calling. Being empowered to leap on the pathway to activating their dream and pursuing it with every part of their life.

As the vision of the Calling settled into my heart, I knew that I would utilize it to create my senior project while also fulfilling God's calling on my life. At only eighteen years old, I walked hand in hand with God to see His dream fulfilled. I had faith that God was true to do what He had promised.

In the class you were only supposed to spend 15 hours of time on the project. Instead, I spent over 240 hours working on the project.

I defined my class project as a Christian event which inspired and motivated attendees to go after their God-given calling. This effort included educating myself, planning and praying as the day of the big event arrived with national artists, speakers and several nonprofits and businesses. I even had to build up the bravery to call the national K-LOVE radio station to help. The regional manager at the time, Jen Lohman answered and believe in the vision God placed on my heart. She was gracious enough to participate and support the event. God was opening up a dynamite network. It was the first gathering, but somewhere deep down in my heart, I was convinced that this wouldn't be the last. It was what I was born to do. My senior project concluded with The Calling's first event. It was amazing and I knew in my heart that it would be the first of many more to come.

The concept of calling is of great importance! It can take you in different directions at various seasons of your life. It could be sparked by one of the sweetest moments of your life or God may show you something to act on by getting your attention in a sorrowful moment. It could be a funeral or the birth of a loved one. It could occur in the midst of your greatest struggles or perhaps be revealed in an everyday routine, like reading this book.

What matters the most is recognizing that God is trying to communicate with you in the unique way that you hear Him. It is imperative that you live out your calling. Your calling holds the power to change the world and turn you into a history maker.

We are all history makers; it just looks different for each person. All callings have a chance to ripple out and touch lives around the world and build God's kingdom. If you have a calling to influence millions of people it is just as powerful as influencing one. Who knows if that one person you are called to serve is the next Billy Graham or Martin Luther King Jr.? Obedience to God is the key to reach your true potential.

After learning about how God revealed my calling, I wouldn't be surprised if you might be wondering, *who is this girl to talk about all of this? Why is she talking about all of this?* Well, truth be told, I am just an ordinary girl. I realize that what I am about to share with you is not normal, it is evidence of a supernatural God living in a simple girls' life. I am one who has experienced extreme frightening and extraordinary events in my life and I don't take them for granted. For God has molded my character through all of them. From being a finalist of ABC's The Bachelor to being Colorado's Choice for Miss Colorado Miss America, to a survivor of Lyme's disease and earthquakes and hurricanes and starting a non-profit at the age of 18 years old. I am the girl who had traveled to Haiti seven times to bring the message of The Calling to the world's most impoverished and even to inside of the White House. I have had opportunities to be Alumni President at Colorado Christian University, American's Top 20 Young Women Entrepreneurs, to the youngest female to produce an event with Grammy Award Entertainment at Red Rocks Amphitheater. All to say, I have seen God do the miraculous time and time again. All of these experiences have not only shaped me and taught me about what God wanted me to grow into. It gave me stepping stones to confirm my calling. Living your calling can come from not only positive situations, but hardships, trials and situations where you are completely outside of your comfort zone.

Many times we don't know why God has placed us in certain situations, but He always connects the dots for a bigger purpose than that moment, even in some of our worst nightmares. Every single inch of you, every single cell and every bit of your spirit becomes aligned to make sure that you execute the calling God has placed on your heart. It begins from within and the feeling is almost indescribable. God gives you His peace to take a step and to know you are not meant to give up no matter how hard your circumstances become.

You feel God around you. You feel that there is something pushing you towards action and not just pushing, but giving, you a heart full of Heavenly courage. Of course, who else but God to give us the head start we need! He chose me for a mission and He has a mission just for you too.

Saying yes to your calling is not just a one-time thing. My mission is confirmed and furthered every time I say yes to the great I Am, the Almighty, Jesus, to being involved in my life and bring Heaven to Earth. And now God is using me to call and inspire you to live out your true God-given dream, this world needs you!

WERE THEY UNWISE OR JUST BOLD TO DARE TO CHANGE HISTORY?

*"Here's to ... the misfits, the rebels, the troublemakers, the round pegs in the square holes ... the ones who see things differently—they're not fond of rules ... You can quote them, disagree with them, glorify or vilify them, but the only thing you can't do is ignore them because they change things ... They push the human race forward, and while some may see them as the odd, we see genius because the ones who are wild enough to think that they can change the world are the ones who do." -***Steve Jobs**

Have you wondered what prompted Jobs to say this? In looking into Steve Jobs' life, we see that Apple was worth $1.5 billion in 1995. In 1996, Jobs negotiated a breakthrough deal with two of the world's most influential companies, Pixar and Disney.

That spring, Apple's board of directors rehired Jobs to be the company's CEO after kicking him out of his own company years before. Not long after his return, he delivered his famous speech about the wild ones – those who dare to think the unthinkable.

Now, I have to ask you how you would feel if you were in Jobs' shoes. How would being kicked out of the company you helped build impact your life, path and identity? Would you feel betrayed? Would you keep going?

For Jobs, the overwhelming feeling was one of freedom. He never stopped pursuing his vision of bringing computers to the masses. When he returned to Apple, he could speak from first-hand experience of being a wild one. He'd had his path rerouted, but persevered anyway, believing in himself and in his calling.

Now ask yourself: *How has God rerouted me? And how will I react?* By understanding that both positive and negative events can shape our lives, we can come to realize that rerouting may turn out to be a gift that you would not otherwise receive. This is the brilliant 'foolishness' that people often attribute to people that are willing to take risks to do something great or follow what God is calling them to do like Walt Disney and Steve Jobs.

The society we live in is very appreciative of people who live by the book, follow all the long-standing norms and dare to not step outside the realm of the "ordinary." It's one where children are taught to reach for the stars, but criticized for dreaming "too big." It is one where kids are punished for trying to find loopholes to bend the rules; and being the black sheep in a flock of white, is heavily frowned upon.

The irony lies in the fact that it's almost always those black sleep, aka "unwise" people, who make a groundbreaking impact on the world. The Founder of Apple, Steve Jobs, was a firm believer in the fact that being a "wild one" was more of an asset than a liability. He believed that in order for us to grow as a society, we must be willing to think outside the box and make decisions others may perceive as odd.

Take a minute to really ponder over it. Think about how much the world has evolved over the last few centuries. Would it ever have been possible if the inventors of impeccable technologies weren't daring enough to challenge the way things were done? Throughout history, if nobody ever stood up in a seated crowd, brought forth an idea unlike any other, we would still be living in a stone age.

A noteworthy example of this is when people found out that Thomas Edison was working on developing the first practical electric light bulb, he was mocked by countless people. In the words of a chief engineer for the British Post Office, *"subdivision of the electric light is an absolute ignis fatuus."* In other words, he stated that it was nothing more than a fairy tale. This one example, goes a long way to reiterate how the people whose names are imprinted in the history books today are those who were ridiculed for their seemingly absurd ideas[1].

When a big portion of America tried to prevent the emancipation of slavery, Abraham Lincoln was daring enough to take a stand in the face of injustice. His plan to end slavery was naturally faced with staunch opposition. Yet, he did not back down. He believed that the cause he was fighting for was worthwhile and meaningful. His determination made him victorious and led to the abolition of the same slavery atrocity that Tubman fought against.

It's hard to imagine in today's world what it would be like to stand up for what was right when the consequences could have cost her life. In 1955, in the South, it was illegal for a Black person to ride in front of a bus. Rosa Parks was the first black woman to object to this preposterous restriction

---

[1] *"It is our attitude at the beginning of a difficult task which, more than anything else, will affect its successful outcome." –* **William James.**

by refusing to move to the back of the bus one historic day in Alabama. She knew her action would not be consequential and that she would be arrested – but she did it anyway. She did not fear the repercussions of challenging the law because she knew that somebody had to stand up in the face of inequity. She understood that making a difference almost always comes with a cost. Today, her name is resonated throughout our history books.

Another notable historic "rebel" was a man whose teachings were objected to by the Roman governor, Pontius Pilate. Regardless of the opposition he faced, that man refused to stop spreading the word of revelation, kindness, empathy and salvation. He stood by his principles fearlessly, even when it endangered his life. That valorous man was, of course, Jesus Christ. His ultimate calling and willingness to be crucified is what launched a global revolution, one so impactful that it's still ongoing after 2000 years, changing the lives of billions of people for eternity.

So, let me ask you this now – were these people foolish or were they just bold? Were they insane as deemed by society at that time or were they just audacious? How different would the world be today if those brave pioneers never stood up for what they believed in? What would history look like if they chose the easy way out instead? What if they succumbed to the societal pressure and gave up on meaningful causes?

The blatant truth is that all of us have an opportunity to have our names written in history. However, just because the world has evolved doesn't mean people don't still feel alienated by somebody who brings forth an unheard idea. If we want to leave behind a legacy, we must be bold enough to strive for greatness, despite knowing the cost. People will perhaps label us negatively, but we have to know that the cause we're fighting for is grander than their criticism or lack of belief. We just have to possess the power of purpose. By doing so our names echo throughout the ages for God's glory.

It is amazing how much our God wants to help us. He has made sure we will reach the destination that He has intended for us. We just need to have that fire within – the willingness to pursue God's plan for us! Yes, the child-like faith to live out our calling! Think about Martin Luther King and the phenomenal legacy he left. Of course, it wasn't easy, and it was something that endangered his life continually, but God kept him going because this was his God-given calling. He didn't just fulfil his calling but, through his calling, changed the world. He changed how an entire race was looked at, and until date, he receives credit for doing for humanity that many others struggled to do. All of this could be well possible because God kept his mighty yet affectionate hand alongside his hands.

THE POWER OF GOD'S PURPOSE

The fountain of youth has yet to be truly found, however, science has shown that having a calling and profound purpose leads to a sufficient amount of years in one's life. None of us are born knowing what the exact plan God has for us, but He will reveal the next step and at the right milestones He will reveal an over-arching theme. He wants us to live for and fight for His glory. The purpose of the 'theme' will mean everything to us and will influence the world around us because His unshakeable truth. Sure, in the process, we sometimes find ourselves being hurt and frustrated, but there isn't anything to worry about. The good news is that God brings full redemption to any situation. I have learned over time that God's redemption brings with it, great love and an epic story. I have experienced that I can and will overcome the harshest of circumstances. The key is having Jesus' lens on the situation.

April 11th 2007 was a momentous day, a day in my history book. As a high school senior I couldn't be more thrilled as the details of my senior project came together. The first conference was held at a church in Littleton, Colorado. More than 250 people attended. That day, God instilled in many people their callings, demonstrating that His message of purpose is for everyone. People were reminded of Jesus Christ's love for them and got a chance to be reconciled with Him for all eternity. They were then asked and challenged with The Calling's message and theme question, "What would you do if you knew you could not fail?"

Most notably after The Calling's 1st gathering, God activated the dream of a 5-year-old girl with cancer who started a club at her elementary school to help other kids with cancer. On the other end of the age spectrum, an 87-year-old man attended the conference and found his calling and started a game night at his nursing home. Everyone there was a child of God and needed only to step forward and follow Jesus' calling for them in all aspects of their lives. There is so much that happened. Some may say or think that this was just a school project, but because God was in it, it was so much more! This 'project' confirmed my calling. I am writing this book over 14 years later knowing that I will be running this ministry with the goal in mind to help others live their calling for all of my days.

From that first conference, things changed drastically. Now fast forward to a few years later, there I was, hosting a massive event at the legendary Red Rocks Amphitheatre, sharing the message the Lord gave me years prior walking down that hall in high school. What was a mere dream of a high school girl became my reality as a senior in college. My God-given dream came true! From a little senior project where He called me out to do something just like this. My mission was accomplished and just beginning.

In hindsight, little had I known that God would grow this dream into what it has become a global non-profit touching hearts across vast cultures and backgrounds. God continued to answer my prayer of showing the world that nothing is impossible when we follow Jesus fearlessly. God had my back the entire time and as I walked on the oath he set for me He continued to whisper to my heart the next steps. Empowered by God's strength, the message of The Calling became more clear, influential and people longed to hear it. The fierce passion within my heart from high school and college transformed The Calling to be a sacred ministry destined to spread hope to the world.

And such is my story of finding my life's purpose. If you don't know yours already expect yours to be revealed to you even when reading this very sentence! Everyone has a calling and God will show you what it is if only you ask Him! Everyone's calling is different, but we are meant to help and support one another. Trust me when I say this; you will be amazed by what you will do, but never thought possible when you leap into your God-given destiny!

Have faith and look up to the Lord as you wait to realize your calling! When you do you will be shown what Heaven is like. Yes, true Heaven on Earth. Once that happens, you will easily move into the purpose God designed just for you, yes, possibly to do even in Heaven.

I found it. Others have found it. You will find it!

You were born to be God's dreamers and a true History maker.

CHAPTER 2

Work to Do in Heaven

Work to do in Heaven

"Oh Darling Heaven has a plan for you!"

Have you ever asked God what your job is going to be in Heaven? God has given you an extraordinary job just for you! When you think about what you would love to do in Heaven, what would that be?

Do you want to be in charge of leading sailboats in Heaven down the rapids of the River of Life? Perhaps you want to sing with the Angelic Choir Tour, going from galaxy to galaxy? Or maybe you want to be Heaven's Top Chef, baking up the best marshmallow cloud tarts? Maybe build a massive treehouse in the Tree of Life? Or become a mighty warrior in Heaven's army?

Or maybe you want to join me in helping Heaven's creation dream and create like never before? I mean if we can build rockets, roller coasters, make cheesecake and soar in airplanes can you imagine what we can also create in Heaven?

My dream is to bring people, angels and all God's creation to massive conferences that star the likes of Jesus and perhaps Michael the Archangel? Imagine Jesus and Michael conducting a conversation for more than a billion people:

Michael says in a T.D. Jake's tone, "Hey Jesus, could you send us some Angels down here? These people reading these words are changing the world and need our backup!"

Jesus replies, "Michael, you asked, and you shall receive."

Michael exclaims, "Does my God deliver or does my God deliver? Yes, my God delivers!" And all the angels applaud with their wings and the clouds of fireworks invading all of the universes stars.

I believe with all my heart that our generation as a whole is meant to change the world in respect to changing our mindset to dream bigger than ever before. This comes from knowing we are meant to start living out our Heavenly callings right now, for such a time as this.

Now, if we really believe in the Bible completely and unequivocally, we need to know that it is in Jesus that we find our true unique purpose. Colossians 1:16-17 says about Jesus, "For in Him all things were created: things in Heaven and on Earth, visible and invisible, whether thrones or powers or rulers or authorities; all things have been created through Him and for Him. He is before all things, and in Him, all things hold together."

Jesus did not leave us without a road map! He gave us the Bible and the Holy Spirit to lead and guide us. He wants to be our ultimate friend to guide us through life's ups and downs. He will lead us to what our true Heavenly destiny is supposed to be. My friends, it is time to think, imagine and believe bigger than you ever have before!

We are talking about the God who created whales to swim in oceans, tuxedos on penguins, dots on ladybugs and even on Dalmatians! He even gave chameleons the ability to change colors and also put dreams in your heart.

This is the time to live out our God-given dreams! Jesus said we would be doing greater things than He to display His magnificent glory to all creation (John 14:12 ESV). Therefore, let us create His dreams like never before! Jesus has huge dreams and He drops them in each of our hearts to live out for His glory.

We can learn from Judges chapter 6, verse 11 (ESV):

"The angel of the Lord came and sat down under the oak in Oprah that belonged to Josh the Abiezrite, where his son Gideon was threshing wheat in a winepress to keep it from the Midianites. When the Angel of the Lord appeared to Gideon, he said, "The Lord is with you, mighty warrior."

Picture a man in the middle of his work. An angel appears to him and declares his entire identity. The key ingredient to living courageously is knowing that God is with you.

The story continues:

"Pardon me, my lord," Gideon replied, "but how can I save Israel? My clan is the weakest in Manasseh, and I am the least in my family."

The Lord answered, "I will be with you and you will strike down all the Midianites, leaving none alive."

Gideon replied, "If now I have found favor in your eyes, give me a sign that it is really you talking to me. Please do not go away until I come back and bring my offering and set it before you." And the Lord said, "I will wait until you return!"

Gideon comes to realize that he had been talking to God all along. Gideon was known for being the weakest in the clan and couldn't believe that God would have a great purpose for him. But by listening and coming to God face to face, his soul was filled with great courage and purpose. This is how he found his true calling and how we can find our own![2]

Heaven coming to Earth happens when we request that God comes down and helps us walk in faith. The Holy Spirit and God's angels are waiting, just as they did with Gideon, to help us and build courage in us.

Hebrews 11:6 reminds us that "… it is impossible to please God without faith." This verse explains that God's great desire for us is to walk by faith.

---

[2] *"I can't change the direction of the wind, but I can adjust my sails to always reach my destination."*– **Jimmy Dean**

GOD'S ROADMAP TO YOUR TRUE CALLING IN HEAVEN

Two legitimate questions to lead us to our true Heavenly calling are, "What is my life's calling?" and "What is God's plan for my life?" As mere mortals, we don't know what is written for our future and what the real plans are thus we must ask God to reveal His plan for us every day. Of course, we do sometimes make our own plans and try to execute them as best we can. What remains a fact is that our plans of doing things on our own come out empty compared to what Jesus truly has in store for us. If we are honest with ourselves, we have all been in that situation and God's grace is amazing enough to get us back on track on His divine treasure map. God's treasure map is the one where we walk with Him to discover His plan for us.

Our calling is particularly related to the deepest desires of our hearts – yes, our dreams. As Psalm 34:7 (ESV) says, 'Delight in me and I will give you the desires of your heart.' When we delight in, praise, honor and surrender to Jesus the desires that land in our hearts are meant to come true. Our dreams and Heaven are a match made in, well, Heaven! We are crafted and designed to live out our dream forever. We aren't just meant to live out our callings here on Earth, but for all eternity. Therefore, you should delight yourself in Jesus right now and then ask yourself again: What do you want your job title to be in Heaven?

God has created the answer to this question to be what we are meant to do now on Earth and forever in Heaven. This is our true calling. When we know what God has planned for us, we see that nothing can stop the dream from coming true except ourselves.

The way our callings will be fulfilled will be you trusting God alone. Isn't it great to know that this is not a variable situation and not dependent on anyone but you. Imagine your life as a garden and in that garden planted in the ground are the seeds of dreams. These seeds are God's dreams from His heart placed inside of you. How you water it, cultivate it and protect it will determine how soon and if your calling will be fulfilled into a 'tree of life' as Proverbs 12:13 describes, 'A hope deferred makes a heart sick but a longing fulfilled is a tree of life.' In various other translations the word 'longing' can also mean dream, purpose, calling.

The God of the Universe and all creation continues to put dreams in our hearts and we are destined to live them out! We have the choice to either live out the dream or pass up the opportunity by letting fear be our leader. This is why I often ask people the theme question of The Calling all the time: What would you do if you knew you could not fail? This question allows people the space to hear God's dream for their lives.

GOD, HIMSELF IS A WORKER

Billy Graham shared many concepts about working in Heaven. The idea of working in Heaven is foreign to many people. Yet, the scripture clearly teaches this concept. When God created Adam, he "took the man and put him in the Garden of Eden to work it and take care of it" (Genesis 2:15). Work was part of the original Eden and it was part of a perfect human life.

God, Himself is a worker. He didn't create the world and then retire. Jesus said, "My Father is always at His work to this very day and I. too, am working" (John 5:17). Jesus found great satisfaction in His work. "'My food,' Jesus said, 'is to do the will of Him who sent me and to finish His work'" (John 4:34).

We also have work to do, satisfying and enriching work that we can't wait to get back to. Work that will never be drudgery. God is the primary worker and as His image-bearers we're made to work. We create, accomplish, set goals and fulfill them—to God's glory!

THE GREAT REFLECTION

Now, we must look into the real question and the primary purpose of this chapter:

Are there any similarities between our 'work' on Earth and in Heaven?

Prior to giving a definite answer, let us first jump into the wonder of God's creation inside the Garden of Eden. Beth Moore (an evangelist and creator) clarifies in her Bible study 'Chasing Vines' that in Genesis, it was God's imagination that enlivened Him to envision Heaven. God formed mankind to work and administer the land. He talked and things came to be.

At the point when God went through six days of planning and developing the world, He conjured up the entirety of the Heavens and the Earth, including all the magnificence around us like the majestic landmasses, the sky, time, warm-blooded creatures, birds in the clouds and all the fish in the ocean. God needed to make an impermanent yet ideal home for all creation that felt like home. Regularly, when I move to another spot, go to a friend's home or even visit a café, I like making the space feel like home. This is exactly what God did. He made Earth have many similarities of Heaven. In the earliest reference point, God made the Garden of Eden as a reflection for Heaven.

There is the Tree of Life in Heaven and God made there a Tree of Good and an Evil in the Garden in Eden. The River of Life referenced in Heaven is additionally found in the Garden of Eden. God was kind enough to make Earth feel like home. This understanding and the application can be seen throughout the Bible as well.

Jesus clearly stated that He wanted us to pray and live out 'Thy Kingdom Come, thy Will be done, on Earth as it is in Heaven (Matthew 6:10 ESV)!' I would say that Heaven coming to Earth looks the most vivid to the people around us when we are living out our true callings. We are meant to be walking around full of life, passionate and thrilled knowing that anything at any moment one can have an impact for the Kingdom to then have a ripple effect for all eternity. You see God desires for the world to be a reflection of our eternal home, Heaven. He even set it up to be like our Heavenly home.

God was making Earth in the image of Heaven. You see in the Garden of Eden God destined Adam to work. This wasn't by accident; this was God's perfect plan. Adam was made to work the land, to name animals to do something that only he was destined to do. We each have a unique purpose to live out if we are willing to leap into God's desire for Heaven. This was God's best plan. When we are working, living out our true calling's we are bringing Heaven to Earth like never before.

In Heaven, we know that anything is possible with God. So why can't this be true here on Earth too?

Have you ever thought that God intended Earth to become even more like Heaven as each of us live out our Heavenly Callings? The very idea that you wonder and think about God and His creation shows that Heaven awaits us and that we have a lot to look forward to doing in Heaven. Can you imagine all the amazing events that will be taking place? Perhaps instead of the Kentucky Derby as we know it, it will be the Heaven Derby featuring the Angels racing one another? Or instead of the super bowl it will be all of Heavens creation playing for a special trophy? The list could go on and on. What does your mind think of wanting to do in Heaven?

Hebrews 11:6 reminds us that "…it is impossible to please God without faith." This verse explains that God's great desire for us is to walk by faith and live out all the dreams He has placed inside of us.

Again I will ask you what do you want your job title to be in Heaven? This answer most likely will profoundly move you closer into your God-given purpose and calling! We are meant to live out our Heavenly jobs here on Earth. You don't have to wait to die to truly live, your moment is now to reflect Heaven.

I want you to think of what you want to do in Heaven forever because this is most likely what you are supposed to be doing here on Earth. When your goals both in Heaven and on Earth align, that's how you know you've found your true calling!

Here are some scriptures to dive in and see God's heart about Heaven, Revelation 22:3, John 5:17, and 1 John 3:2.

CHAPTER 3
Living Out Your Calling

> Belief in someone's calling is a simple gift to give, but it has the power to ripple out and change the world to be like Heaven!
>
> —Chrysandra Brunson

The hope of a unique calling really does give every soul wings to soar and do the seemingly impossible. A calling is as essential as water and food are for the body. If we do not believe we have a special mission to live for our life goes from adventurous and thrilling, to dull and boring. God is the author of dreams and the ultimate dreamer. This is why I believe He has put The Calling's message in front of Presidents, Prime Ministers, Archbishops, country music stars, rap stars, philanthropists, you name it and even on world-famous stages. God is creating the ultimate network for the world to know and see that no dream of God's is too big or small. Every person has been created out of a dream and with a dream. The fact that you are reading this book is proof that God has the most EXTRAORDINARY dream for you to live out!

You were a dream in God's heart. He dreamt up the laugh you would have, the smile you could give, a heart you would have to beat His loving anthem. Yes, you were and are God's dearest dream. Within you He placed dreams to live out for His glory. This is your true calling. Again, God's dreams within you are a person's true calling! You have God's dreams laying within you. What are you going to do with these Heavenly treasures?

It is time to live out the dream He has given you and make the most out of every moment. Once we understand that it is God who controls the tiniest particle in the universe, to the smallest pieces of sand we know we can trust Him. The sooner we act upon it; the sooner we will find it for ourselves. God knows you and knows the perfect dream to put inside your heart. Your age, background, culture and perspective are all meant to help you plunge into the sea of possibilities within your calling.

Don't make it complicated. God made it simple to find your calling. It is beaming within your heart!

NOW WHAT IS A CALLING?

Now it must be asked: **What do you really believe a calling is?** Is it something that gets your heart excited? Or is it a career, ministry, business or random idea? Is it a role that you feel compelled to fulfill in a person's life, your family or your community? It could be a mix of of these aspects and more. After all, what is your life without a purpose to live out? If you cannot answer these questions now that is okay, but I encourage you to look at your life and ask yourself what is meaningful to you?

If you are still trying to figure what your purpose is do not worry. If you ask God to show you and expect Him to reveal it to you in His time it will happen! Consider your experience during a major tragedy or loss. What was meaningful to you during this time? When you got through it what is one thing that God taught you about who He is or yourself? With this question answered is there something that you need to pursue or change as a result? God always shows us in scripture and circumstances He is faithful.

Even someone that has become your biggest hero has had to intentionally pursue their *calling*. Everyone has a calling and this doesn't have to be a calling with a large bank account or even be acknowledged by others. God has assigned you to do something great. The fact that you picked up this book is the only sign you need to know God has a calling for your life and you will live it out. God's timing is always perfect and although you may have been taught about Jeremiah 29:11 (ESV) you may or may have not received it for yourself or put it into action. God wants to prosper you and he has a plan for your future! If you haven't done it before, your time is now! When you seek God with all your heart, you will discover his plan for you!

If we wait to act on what God is telling us to do we run the risk of derailment. We should not wait until tomorrow, or the day after, or the weekend to act upon our callings. If God is revealing your calling now the chances are high that He has orchestrated all the other factors in this moment to fulfill your calling. This includes the people, the open doors and even the exact amount of finances you need to take the next step in your calling. Callings start with God, then us, and almost usually always include others! They take resources, time and selflessness to achieve.

ACT IMMEDIATELY

As soon as you recognize your calling, it is important to act upon it immediately. Do not wait until tomorrow, next week, next year, but now! God is moving in our world like never before to shake up and burst forth the true world changers. The dream hidden and woven within your heart is meant to come alive for such a time as this. God is so good that He will regularly remind you of His calling for you too. Either way, to have to live by your calling is the real deal, the primary purpose of your existence.

Living out your calling has the power to cause a ripple effect and transform lives around the globe. That's why you should never underestimate someone's dream – especially your own! Your calling is the best gift you can give humanity; you must live it out. The key is to live out a small piece of the dream every day, starting right now. There cannot be enough emphasis on all of this, to be fair, because what is our life without its defined purpose, right?

GOD'S WORK

Remember that you do not need to be a pastor, evangelist or hold any similar position before God can use your calling. As believers our goal is to make Jesus known to others, help others grow their faith in God, and help them to the best of your ability in whatever capacity you find yourself in. Every one of your actions will thread into your calling. The key is to tie the small and the large vision together. As Paul says, *'do all to the glory of God* (1 Corinthians 10:31).

God cares more about who we are becoming to see our individual calling's fulfilled. It is vital that we capture every opportunity to love and care for others wherever we go for God's glory. Suppose you have discovered that your calling is to bring hope and healing to others. Well, to begin with, that is an absolutely noble calling! However, what does that really mean? God cares about the details, He wants to color that in for you. He doesn't want to give you a rough streak, but a vivid brilliantly colored master piece to go by. Start writing down the vision you see for your life. When it comes to its implementation, you can achieve that goal either by encouraging others through counseling, becoming a physician, engineer, scientist, worship leader, entrepreneur to create healing machines, etc. All of your actions are in line with your calling. There is more to your calling than having a job title or a position in church; calling is more about the mission that redefines our service to God and people, a way of life.

Now when you are reading this story you are hearing from me, a girl, who has experienced all kinds of unlikely life events. I am just a girl whose world was transformed by King Jesus, a girl whose calling is to inspire others to live out their true God-given dream.

My life has found fierce passion, holy confidence and divine calling when hearing a whisper from God's heart to mine. One of the most memorable whispers occurred during my high school senior year. I was walking to my next class while others ran by me to beat the tardy bell. I then heard a stern, calm, soothing voice that miraculously captured my attention and stopped me amidst the chaos: "Tell them not to be afraid, for I am with them."

This was my calling, God's work for me to do. It is my hope and dream that you are inspired to live out your calling through reading about my life experiences. If I can do it, anyone can, especially you!

BEHIND THE SCENES OF A NORMAL GIRL

"Don't ever let anyone tell you that you cannot go after your dream, not even me. You got a dream, protect it. When people can't do it for themselves, they are going to tell you that you can't do it. You want something, go get it. Period!" - Will Smith, in 'The Pursuit of Happiness

Am I the only one that cried like a baby watching Pursuit of Happiness for the first time or every time! Ha, the power of this movie showcasing the determination it takes to live out our dreams is priceless. My heart has deeply resonated with this passion and conviction that nothing must stop the dreams deep within my heart. I believe this fierce passion lies in your heart too.

As I have lived my life, I have come to realize I was born to dream. Since as far back as I can remember, I have asked the Lord multiple times to be His beloved dreamer. The Lord has answered my call, slowly but surely, with plenty of bumps along the way. From the time when I had one cent in my bank account to a crashing computer wiping out years of work, it all had been worth it. I've witnessed the Prime Minister of Australia address the youngest person ever to sail around the world; I've witnessed the Pope addressing the United States Congress and I've been invited to the United States presidential inaugural ball; I've been truly blessed mostly with the peace of God's presence in my life.

As God's children, we are each meant to be Heaven's dreamers in our sphere of influence. We were born to make the most out of every opportunity with a servant's heart. As Jesus commanded:

Making the most of every opportunity because the days are evil (Ephesians 5:16).

What has helped me push forward through the challenges I have faced is God's great 'head nod.' It's that feeling of a divine whisper that reminds one that they are meant to do something great! He gives you holy confidence to plow through whatever barriers lie in front of you. We were born to be the dreamers of the world. "The era we are living in today is a dream coming true!" - Walt Disney

We are destined to live out our dreams for the future that God desires possible. Not only for ourselves but our future families, communities, nation and the entire world! YOU can change the world. YOU can change yourself. YOU can live your dreams. YOU can do all of that with God's hand settled comfortably in yours.[3]

HOW I FOUND THE CALLING AND THE CALLING FOUND ME

As I live my calling today, it is imperative that I talk about the way the calling found me and I found it. Hopefully this will kindle up inspiration for you to use your background to live your calling. Our callings come to us like magnets.

I am often bewildered that God sent the dream of the calling from His heart to mine. Out of all the ordinary people in this world, I humbly know there are tons of other extremely more qualified people that God could have picked to put this dream of The Calling from his heart into the world. However, when I think back to my early childhood, I can reminisce God transmitting His purpose for me, the same way that He has for you!

Even in the meaning of my name, I can see God's influence. Before I was born, my parents, Karen and Phil, were notified by the 1980's doctors ultrasound that I would be a boy. Yep, they painted my room blue, had a boy baby shower and bought lots of boy baby clothes especially as the first born baby of the family. So yes, at the time of my birth it was quite a surprise and shock that surely you can imagine. The doctor announced, "It's a girl!" After the numerous body checks and laughs my parents realized the boy names they were thinking of were just not going to work out so well so they started brainstorming. They finally created my name,

---

[3] *"Courage is resistance to fear, mastery of fear, not absence of fear."* -**Mark Twain**

Chrysandra. They combined the magic of Christmas, Chrysanthemums and the element of surprise into my name. I love that they made it up, as that completely suits my personality for I love coming up with new ideas and imagining God's best for all situations.

Later, I would also find out what Chrysandra means. Chrys comes from Christine, meaning Christ-bearer. Sandra means helper of humanity. Altogether, Chrysandra means Christ-bearer as helper of humanity! I have never met another Chrysandra, but I hope to one day. God knows each of us by name even before we're born; He had created each of us with a magnificent plan to fulfill His purpose and knows us by name even before our parents name us!

My entire childhood was an adventure and my parents ensured that we were well-taken care of in every aspect of our lives. God even gave me a sister and forever best friend, Brittany Elizabeth Brunson, just fourteen months later. God knew that Britt and I would need each other through all of life's adventures, full of ups and downs. We were both born with kindness, optimism and zeal in our souls.

When I was two and a half, Brittany, our friend and I, watched Peter Pan for the first time. We loved it immediately, and I knew what I needed to do after watching it. I called a kid meeting in my room. I declared that if Peter Pan and Wendy could fly, I could too. Most the kids assured me I could definitely not fly but a couple of friends believed I could. What did I do? Did I step away wisely? Oh no. I climbed on top of my seven-foot dresser and jumped with my arms wide open. Did I fly? No, I did not. However, I did break my arm while trying. I quickly found out why my tactic did not work—I had forgotten Tinkerbell's pixie dust. This goes along with a life moto I have tried to live by all my days, "Shoot for the moon and if you miss, at least you'll be among the stars." I believe that we were each born to have this sense of fearlessness.

In fact, my whole family has always craved adventure. My mom taught us to live each day to the fullest. When it was chore time, we would blast country music, especially Trisha Yearwood's "X's & O's," and sing and dance while we cleaned.

And speaking of my mom, she was our pillar and real-life wonder woman. She took us on countless adventures that created a foundation in my sister and I's hearts to see the world through the wondrous eyes of God.

She was also an Anatomy & Physiology, Biology, teacher at the high school and university level. Believe it or not, she was Brittany and I's teacher in high school too. She loved God and taught us to always look to Him for answers and comfort. The more I think about it, the more I realize that this longing for God and His message came to me from my parents. Who believed that God gave us the best of both worlds, the temporary one here and the permanent one up there. They taught the importance of putting Jesus first in everything for He was the only one that we could always count on.

To speak of our dad, I owe it to him for stretching our horizons on what was possible while also keeping us grounded. He even created a movie theatre in the basement with shooting stars that streamed across the ceiling and a pond in the backyard that is larger than most swimming pools all by himself. In his creativity he built in bronze dolphins shooting out water of their mouths, always going above and beyond to make an event, day or landscape extra special. As a rocket engineer working for Locked Martin and NASA, my dad loved bringing me to *'Take Your Daughter to Work Day,'* where we'd discover all about space and the glorious beauty of God's heart within the universe. My dad always went above and beyond to make every moment count when we were all together. My dad would always maximize our time together from compacting a 2-hour time frame to combine puzzles, Pretty Pretty Princess, swimming, soccer, tree climbing and maybe homework. We would go sledding late at night and roller skating down steep hills on grass on gorgeous Colorado summer days. These moments created in me my fearless attitude to not only have the guts to ride a scary roller-coaster 10 times in a row at a young age to then have the courage to speak in front of 40,000 people in the middle of the night. Being stretched outside my comfort zone as a child has made it a lifestyle as an adult.

My sister, Brittany, and I grew up knowing that dreams could become a reality with hard work, kindness, and an imaginative heart, knowing that nothing is impossible with God. Brittany has been my forever best friend and as shown me what God means when it comes when He says He wants to be our best friend at all times. She has been my best friend since being in my mama's womb. Having her in the best of times and worst of life's ventures knowing that she was always there for me and willing to do anything to help, love, support, encourage and believe in me has been the best gift anyone could ever have. I would often have bullies growing up that would say mean things, leave me out and even mock me. Brittany would always stick up for me and encourage me to keep dreaming and going for all the big dreams in my heart. Her favorite saying is, 'Go Sha-Sha Go!' Sha-Sha is the favorite family nickname that I am often called by. Brittany is using her superpowers of humor, love and healing as an ER nurse and graduated from University with honors in science. She shares God's love with all who know her, but especially with her patients. She just married her soulmate Lance and they are both living out God's calling for their lives fearlessly.

One time when I was ten, my mom took Brittany and I went up to Victoria, Canada. I had saved all my money for a couple of years to go whale watching as I truly do love whales. When we arrived in the city, we boarded a boat and began our adventure to find the whales. But after two hours of no sightings, the captain said he was going to turn the boat around. I pleaded with the captain to stay just a little longer, and he did. Then, just a few minutes later, a pod of Orcas appeared out of nowhere! It was a dream come true. That day, God showed me the value of persistence, power of vision and the excitement of adventure!

However, life wasn't all sweet during childhood. My parents divorced when I was three years old.[4] It has been one of the toughest events I've ever had to overcome. Gas stations and McDonald's took on a different meaning because that's where we would need to do the 'switch' and go from one home to another. We would say goodbye to and hello in the same breath. There are truly no words to share the depths of sorrow that one can feel during such a trial involving two people you love the most. However, I learned to have God's lens on the situation and learned that God was going to give me two families that love me just as much while doubling the love. I can see that this in many ways that this would prepare me for marriage. God used my family especially my parents, sister, brothers, step-parents, Nana, Papa, Grandma, Grandpa, Aunts, Uncles and Cousins to love and support me and make me who I am today.

---

[4] *"Most of the important things in the world have been accomplished by people who have kept on trying when there seemed to be no hope at all."* -**Dale Carnegie**

The reason I am sharing my childhood experience is that it is an experience that many might resonate. Your calling will not come to you when everything is going right in your life, most of the time the rough behind the scenes scenarios create the atmosphere to craft and mold your character into who God has created you to become more than any other situation.

Through these trials, I learned to be resilient and overcome challenges that have helped me to deal with the myriad challenges that life throws our way. My family taught me to truly live life to the fullest and make the most of every situation. I owe it to them for my desire to seek my calling and also the will to execute that calling into truly living it out. One of the greatest gifts my family bestowed upon me is learning the art of taking moments of heartbreak into achieving dreams. In school, that was in athletics and student government. Later on, it was in organizing events that attracted thousands of people and helping people find their calling and achieving their dreams.

You see, all of us dream and when those dreams finally look like they might become a reality, some of the biggest trials may come to hit us and knock us down. However, the good news is that God brings full healing to any situation. I have learned over time that God's redemption brings with it great love. When we have God's perspective on a situation we see real truth, real potential and someone's real calling. I saw that God not only let Brittany and I have one immediate family to love us, but two! I have learned that to overcome harsh circumstances. God allowed my family to grow because of the breakup, as Brittany and I gained a loving stepmom Pam, a loving stepdad Craig, and even two adopted brothers from Ukraine, Max, and Andy. My extended family always ensured that Brittany and I were loved unconditionally and that we never felt responsible for the divorce.

Witnessing the great heartbreaks while growing up set the stage for the largest platforms in my future. So I ask you too, what kinds of childhood heartbreaks did you have? How did they build your character and help you become who you are today? Yes, we might sometimes try to run away from our past, but if we let those heartbreaks grow into compassion and something beautiful, the most painful things in our lives can become our biggest asset. It is essential to understand this in the context of your calling because in pursing your calling you will always have roadblocks that you can never anticipate, but you were destined and made to overcome them.

A LOVE FOR THINKING OUTSIDE THE BOX

Another key characteristic I found about myself is a love for creating. I grew up knowing that in every situation, there are always ways to think outside the box; that a situation can be a little better than when I first saw it. I even remember as a kindergartener and first-grader from Bear Creek Elementary asking for ways to improve my grade on an assignment or asking for an extra family member to come to an event. I always wanted to do as many things as exceptionally well as possible to stretch the limits of my potential. God instilled in me a desire to excel in as many ways as I could. I'd say it is in my DNA. I found that this usually began with asking: first God, then ourselves and finally, the world. Painting a picture for people of what can be was key.

This pattern continued into high school: from being Varsity Cheerleading team captain to a varsity track sprinter, soccer player, vice-president of the National Honor Society, Sophomore and Junior Class President, even becoming Student Body President. I always felt there was room to learn from others and to grow in the 'fish tank' I was in. I have loved knowing both sides of a story knowing that context helps drive the bottom rooted answer needed. I loved seeing that to make things happen it is important to talk to the decision makers, yes the leaders and see how to serve the environment I was in.

A love for leadership and the desire to think outside the box carried me through college. When I couldn't settle on a major that fit my needs, I made one up. That's how *Business Communications* became not only my major but also a future major for others at the University. I combined that major with a minor in Leadership. [5]One of my favorite professors, Dr. Gary Ewen, taught a leadership course on the magic of Disney. This exciting course enabled our class to learn about the company's famous business principles. I asked Dr. Ewen if we could go to Disney to visually see and learn these magical principles. We ended up all going. Now it has been

---

[5] *"It always seems impossible until it's done."*-**Nelson Mandela**

built into the course to this day over 10 years later! We learned about the business principles that Walt Disney put into practice. We were the first class to get that opportunity. Through this, God again showed me the power of asking. I even got my Masters in Business, yes my MBA with a self-designed emphasis called Disney Leadership. This all with the great help of the awe-inspiring world leader and Masters Dean Dr. Mellani Day. She then has believed in me since and has traveled with me to Haiti to spread the message of The Calling. We also created curriculum for The Calling to use on Entrepreneurism.

Of course, I've met my share of bullies and dream deniers along the way, especially in middle school. I went to a pretty small yet prestigious school with three to five hours of homework a night. There were 80 kids in my class and 20 of the girls decided to pick on me. They picked two days in particular where they all wore their hair on top of their heads like me. They left me out of the circle conversations and made me sit at the end of the table for lunch. I would come home every day crying, convinced that they just hated me. My family would continually reassure me that they were just mean girls insecure about themselves, so they were making fun of me. Through the grace of God, I made it through that middle school nightmare and discovered the power of God's glory and my identity in Him in the process. I came to know that as a daughter of God I get to listen to what God says about me and no one else.

GOD CALLS US DAILY

As I mentioned in the earlier chapters, my calling came to me as I walked down the hallway thinking about a senior project that needed to be submitted. The Lord miraculously stopped me in that loud, crowded hallway and clearly said:

"Chrysandra, so many of my children are afraid to go after the things I am calling them to and there is no reason to be afraid. I am right here with you, leading you all the way!"

I continued to listen and started imagining the possibilities that could result if God's people fearlessly embraced His calling into their lives. I started seeing in visions that the world would see Jesus in such a new and vivid way. Then, they will truly know that an abundant life with Jesus Christ is the one in which we were all meant to live and even act every second of our lives.

When we talk about The Calling and how it needs to be implemented in our lives, I can say for sure that God loves taking to us out of our daily routines. Isn't it when you least expect it that you feel and hear God say something in your heart? Chances are you have. Some might say that it is just the conscience speaking. But, my friends if it is noble, honorable, righteous to love God and others that is God talking to you and most likely your calling. It is in His voice that we hear – the calling.

I have come to realize that to live out our callings requires deep intimacy with Jesus in all circumstances. Knowing that He is the reason for all things in Heaven and on Earth. Nothing should get in the way of surrendering to Him allows us to be fearless in the midst of all circumstances.

Challenging people with the question, "What would you do if you knew you could not fail" is a great platform for people to recognize their calling. As I was brainstorming what would be a way for people to truly activate God's calling to them, I imagined the power of having businesses and non-profits on-site to activate people's callings. There is holy power and creativity in community, the sparks of Heaven zoom down to ignite hearts with encouragement and empowerment. I then thought of the integral part of having local churches represented at the conferences. This would allow people to come together with lots of different communities and then return to their home church to live out their callings. The conference would help and direct the people to start, continue and forever live their callings.

Through the activation of individual callings, the church might see people who were teachers become doctors, ambassadors become farmers, veterinarians become secretaries, engineers become social workers, NFL quarterbacks become businessmen. God can have any of His children become anything that He has called them to be in any season of life and at any age. Is that not a beautiful thought to have and begin with? He can give us any dream and yet often times we chase the status quo of what regular adults are supposed to do to be successful, working 9 to 5 and early a few benefits. However, deep down souls are yearning for more than just a job, but their Heavenly purpose to be fulfilled as their job.

TRUST HIM EVERY STEP OF THE WAY

In the pursuit of your calling, there will be plenty of obstacles and giants to overcome along the way. I was hit from all directions by people who didn't believe The Calling could be done and still do every day. I heard such statements as: *"Chrysandra, you will just have to find a smaller group."* Or, *"Chrysandra, you need to stop now—otherwise, you are going to fail in front of everyone!"* Or, *'Chrysandra you will never be able to have The Calling be your full time job.'*

Many questions would often arise in my mind as I thought about the kind of journey I had started. However, all of those questions and doubts began to vanish as I continued to set my eyes on Jesus. Handing my life and decisions into the hands of God has been the most liberating feeling that I ever felt. It is what has truly enabled me to go further than I ever thought possible.

Clearly, this was more than just a school project and as I fast forward The Calling arrived at the point where it was hosting a massive event at the legendary Red Rocks Amphitheater. What appeared to be the impossible of this world became possible with the living, breathing God of the universe!

Little did I know that God would grow this dream birthed from my high school Senior Project course into what has now become a global nonprofit. God continued to answer my prayer of showing the world that nothing is impossible when we follow Jesus fearlessly.

HOW TO TURN MY CALLING INTO MY PROFESSION

My senior project and everything else went as planned and before I knew it, these humble beginnings continued to burn with fierce passion in my heart as I graduated from high school and went to college. I knew that God had continued to put The Calling on my heart, but I didn't know how I would incorporate it into my schooling. I went into college thinking that I would become a teacher. Instead, halfway through my time at University, God spoke to my heart and said:

"Chrysandra, you could be a teacher, and you would love it, but you would always wonder what if?"

I knew right away what that "what if" would be for me: It would be if this dream I had in high school could become my full-time vocation. I prayed about it and God placed it on my heart for it to be so. I could feel in my bones that this is what I was destined for. I knew that I couldn't live with a "what if." I would need to see this through.

What does God want you to do that you find impossible?

The truth is that whatever God wants you to do could be unimaginable, unthinkable and seemingly impossible for you.

However, it will only make sense when you obey and trust Him each step of the way.

God continues to accomplish His purposes here on Earth through countless men and women walking in faith. If you want to be part of such a purpose, be obedient to God and let Him handle the rest.

Seek your calling, live your calling and let God decide for you what you aren't able to. He loves you and He is all-knowing. Trust me! I am telling you this through first-hand experience. I want to encourage what is possible for you. I do not want you to live with any 'what if's,' now is the time to launch into your fullest potential.

YOUR CALLING ISN'T ABOUT YOU

Our mindset is our reality. The reality is that when we ask Jesus Christ to forgive us of our sins and ask Him to lead our lives, He will adopt us as His children and invite us to live out an adventure of a life time. This starts the moment you ask Him into your heart. You then get to spend eternity with Him.

In this entire journey that we take, it is absolutely fundamental that we clear up a few misunderstandings about calling. Your calling certainly isn't about you! You are not called for your own success or gratification, you're called for the good of others and the advancement of God's kingdom here on earth.

Remember that:

"for as in one body we have many members, and the members do not all have the same function, so we, though many, are one body in Christ, and individually members one of another" (Romans 12:4-5).

Moreover, your calling doesn't have to necessarily be your career.

While there might be some overlap between your career and your calling, your career and calling aren't always the same in certain seasons. You can use your job for God's glory even when your calling and profession aren't the same. The third thing to keep in mind is that you don't get to choose your calling, no matter how hard you try. God calls us based on His plan for us. It is His and only His plan that matters in this entire journey. With that being said, He will only call you to something that He has designed you to so do not worry. This is the only way you can have passion to fulfill it.

Let's get to the crux of the matter here and understand what needs to be done to find your calling from God. There is a rather high chance that you have no idea where to start when trying to identify God's plan for you. Nobody does. I mean, do you think people like Amelia Earhart knew what was happening to her when she received her calling to be the first woman to fly across the Atlantic Ocean? The list could go on and on, and you (yes, you), will find yourself on that list as well when you jump into God's plan for you.

HOW DO YOU KNOW IT IS YOUR CALLING

How do you know it is time for your calling and how do you pursue it? Start using your God-given talents and gifts to impact people's lives positively. Do great things to build His kingdom one act at a time. Put others before yourself. And then your calling will be confirmed or redirected. God is the master orchestrator when it comes to loving Him. He will supernaturally line you up to fulfill your destiny.

Regardless of your calling, we as believers are called into a ministry in one way or another. There are plenty of different places within the Bible and in history of the Christian faith that you can find references of. For example, let us look at this verse from the Bible;

"And he gave the apostles, the prophets, the evangelists, the shepherds, and teachers, to equip the saints for the work of ministry, for building up the body of Christ …" (Ephesians 4:11-12)

You can find similar proof here:

"But I do not account my life of any value nor as precious to myself, if only I may finish my course and the ministry that I received from the Lord Jesus, to testify to the gospel of the grace of God" (Acts 20:24).

6 STEPS TO FIND YOUR CALLING

Let's look at six simple and practical steps to find your calling from God. These will help you clear your confusion in regards to your calling.

STEP 1: REMEMBER WHO GOD IS

You have to truly understand who God is and His character. You then you will begin to understand who you are and what you're called to do. Once you begin to know God's character and love for you there is no stopping His plan for you. God will show you through the Bible that He is the same God from Genesis to Revelation and we can trust Him. How can we have deeper understanding of God? The answer is the same as what you would do to get to know a new friend. Spend time with Him!

Read His word and pray. A few ideas are to invest in a devotional, and a prayer journal, make it fun people! Be still and listen to His voice. It isn't easy. However, the more you do it the easier it gets. The more you hear God's direction for your life. God's word is a lamp to our feet and light to our path. Being able to comprehend the most majestic being in the universe might not be the easiest thing to do. But, when you put your heart in it, trust me, He helps you and He gravitates you towards him and reveals truth. Your calling begins with truly knowing the only one who put the dream in you.

GOD'S PLANS ARE BIGGER THAN OUR WAYS

"for my thoughts are not your thoughts, neither are your ways my ways, declares the Lord" (Isaiah 55:8).

HIS LOVE FOR YOU IS FAR GREATER THAN YOU CAN IMAGINE

"See what kind of love the Father has given to us, that we should be called children of God; and so we are. The reason why the world does not know us is that it did not know him" (1 John 3:11).

GOD HAS A PLAN FOR YOUR LIFE

"for I know the plans I have for you, declares the Lord, plans for welfare and not for evil, to give you a future and a hope" (Jeremiah 29:11).

So, take your time to know Him as a friend, a father and your Heavenly King.

STEP 2: KNOW YOUR IDENTITY IN HIM

There is a reason that all of us were born to the world. You will experience significant changes once you know who God is, you will take delight in those truths. Throughout His word, God tells us who He has created us to be. We are chosen, beautiful, handsome, cherished and created in God's image like no one in all the world for such a time as this.

YOU ARE CHOSEN

"But you are a chosen race, a royal priesthood, a holy nation, a people for His possession, that you may proclaim the excellencies of him who called you out of darkness into His marvelous light" (1 Peter 2:9).

GOD'S LOVE FOR YOU REMAINS UNFAILING

"*How precious is your steadfast love, O God! The children of mankind take refuge in the shadow of your wings*" (Psalm 36:7).

YOU'RE BEAUTIFUL

"You are altogether beautiful, my darling; there is no flaw in you" (Song of Songs 4:7).

YOU ARE HIS

"But to all who did receive him, who believed in His name, he gave the right to become children of God …" (John 1:12).

STEP 3: PRAY

Pray to Him always and give Him thanks in all circumstances. Ask the Holy Spirit to reveal Himself to you and He will! He will show you the gifts He has given you and the ways He wants you to use them. Spend time serving others and your calling will find you. You will feel more energy, peace and joy than ever before as you continually submit your ways to Jesus as you will know God's peace over it.

"Is anyone among you suffering? Let him pray. Is anyone cheerful? Let him sing praise" (James 5:13).

"Beloved, I pray that all may go well with you and that you may be in good health, as it goes well with your soul" (3 John 1:2).

STEP 4: PLAN PROPERLY

It is absolutely imperative to plan. Jesus is our guide and He will establish our path. Let's go into a little detail about it.

First list your Talents. Your talents are the natural or developed skills that God has given you to excel in various areas such as teaching, writing, math, graphic design, math, cooking, etc. Ask yourself what brings your soul joy?

Next, identify your gifts in the spirit. Gifts are spiritual areas of life with which God has blessed you. Such gifts may include evangelism, discernment, craftsmanship, administration and hospitality.

Prayerfully answer the following questions. If you could talk about or spend the rest of your life doing one thing, what would it be? What do you love doing?

Your answer to these questions will help you plan and execute.

"The plans of the diligent lead surely to abundance, but everyone who is hasty comes only to poverty" (Proverbs 21:5).

"The heart of man plans his way, but the Lord establishes his steps" (Proverbs 16:9).

STEP 5: SEEK TRUSTED COUNSEL

When making decisions or struggling somewhere in life, you can seek wise counsel. It can be as simple as seeking professional Christian counseling, life coaching, talking with a trusted friend or family member. You want to speak to someone that has God's heart and best interest for you. When things are not clear, these wise counselors can help you to find direction.

Regardless of the person you choose as your trusted counsel, be sure that they have a strong faith and can provide you with the support, discernment and wisdom. If you can't find people like this, keep studying and meditating on God's word until you start receiving instructions through the Holy Spirit.

There is no better counsel than that one that leads you in the way of faith.

"Where there is no guidance, a people falls but in an abundance of counselors there is safety" (Proverbs 11:14).

STEP 6: PRAY MORE

The single most important thing that any believer can do is to pray and keep praying. Our mode of communication is prayer and it is during these conversations, we enjoy a great fellowship time with God. As part of this we share with God and listen to His voice.

The most crucial part of your journey to discovering God's plan in your life is to be intentional with your prayer time about finding God's purpose for you. Carve out time to hear from the Holy Spirit. Write what you would imagine Him saying to you. List scriptures throughout the Bible that resonate with your circumstances. Release all anxiety, fear and requests aside and put them at God's throne room. It is when you have an open heart that you really can hear God's truth and direction. Most of the time He will only reveal the next step. God wants an amazing relationship with you and it is in these constant conversations that the way He has for us is shown. God cannot wait to hear from you! He is waiting, trust me.

A SIMPLE PRAYER TO FIND YOUR CALLING

In the midst, as we talk about praying and what it will bring forth in your life pray this prayer daily as you seek to find your calling:

Jesus, I surrender my life and everything in it to you. Thank you that you are Lord of Lords and King of Kings, my Savior and you want to be my best friend. I want my life to glorify you alone and live out the destiny that you have just for me. I know I can't do this on my own and want you to lead me.

I acknowledge the talents and gifts you've given to me, and I ask that you use me as a mighty pillar and vessel to build your kingdom. Reveal your plan for my life in every step I take.

You tell me in your word not to worry about yesterday, tomorrow or the future but to focus on today. Today, show me where you want me. Show me the unique purpose that you have just for me, and confirm it. Thank you that I don't have to fear stepping out in faith. You are always faithful to confirm my steps and redirect them when needed.

Purify my heart's desires to align with your plan and dare to hear your dreams for my life. Give me your perspective about each decision and love others the same way you have loved me. Give me the faith and courage to follow you fearlessly. I love you.

Allow me to seek you always, hear your call, and obey your voice. Thy Kingdom come thy will be done on Earth as it is in Heaven. Amen.

As you are seeking God's face and see the world through His eyes, you will eventually find your true calling. There is nothing more exciting than being able to understand God's ways and take the path that He has specifically designed for you!

DON'T WAIT TO LIVE OUT YOUR CALLING

Your life and time are too precious to wait to ask these questions. Do not be hesitant to pray and ask God for help to live out your calling. The fact of the matter remains that God has an extraordinary plan for you here on earth and in Heaven. Through the Holy Spirit, God will show you His plan for you.

God made everything on purpose, especially you. Every animal, plant, and especially every human soul has a unique outlook, vision, idea to birth into the world. You are here at a particular moment in time to do something that only you can do to impact the world as only you can.

It is said that the spot filled with the most dreams are those in the cemeteries. For the dreams inside of people's hearts haven't come true and they die with those individuals. Don't let your dreams be buried. Let God breathe life into your calling today. Don't complicate your calling. Ask your heart *What you would do if you knew you could not fail* (#wwydiykycnf) the step out in faith to do it. God has confidence you can do it, so do it. God has trust that you alone can live out His dream, He placed in you. Trust Him to fulfill it!

ALL IN ALL

It is important to know that the singular basis for all activities and goals associated with The Calling is the Gospel of Jesus Christ. This is our recognition that we are actively and naturally inclined to disobey God and the way of life he has prescribed for us. But God, with immense love for us, sent his son Jesus to receive the consequences of our rebellion. If we recognize our need for restoration, we simply need to trust God and trust that Christ's payment was enough. We will again find acceptance with God and are made able to have an active relationship with him. He continues to love us at the depths of who we are with immense strength.

Our response of love to God comes in a very simple form: we obey. First of all, we obey his commandments and his command to love the people around us. Secondly, we obey the direction he gives us in our individual lives. Often, this can be the most difficult area to obey God because it is different for everyone. It is easy to be afraid of being wrong about what we hear him calling us to do. It is a frightening to risk what we have in the present for an unsure future and it is difficult to trust God when we don't have a lot of evidence.

The Calling is not merely about inspiring peoples' dreams to come true – but about helping people understand and achieve the dreams God has given each individual. We trust that God is actively making the world what it needs to be and our role in that process is merely doing what he has asked us to do at an individual level. Your calling from God will never contradict the Gospel of Jesus Christ, the commands God has given us, including his commands to love him and others. We want to help you answer the questions: 1 – what is God calling me to? And 2 – how do I fearlessly obey?

This book and The Calling are here to help you discern what it is God is calling you to and to encourage you to fearlessly obey – if it is God calling, he will not let you fail!

Romans 3:23, John 3:16, John 14:15, Romans 8:28, 2 Peter 1:3-10

CHAPTER 4

How to Turn Your Dreams into Reality

> "What you get by achieving your goals is not as important as what you become by achieving your goals."
> —Zig Ziegler

Isn't it incredible that everything around us started as a dream? The Calling was once a dream. I was once a dream and you were once a dream!

This is how God created and continues to create all things in and through us. Our Heavenly Father says something and it is meant to be lived out. Our God is the ultimate dreamer and He continues to dream every second of every day. He wants to live out these special dreams inside of every one of us. God loves and adores working His good through the beauty of our dreams because they are from Him!

All things in Heaven and Earth were created in Him and through Him. We can only see our true, unique purpose in and through Him. The pastor of National Community Church, Mark Batterson, shares in his book, The Circle Maker, 'Our prayers are like prophesy for our future!' What we dream and pray about becomes our reality!

THE IMPORTANCE OF DREAMING

The world around us doesn't carry much value in the importance of dreaming. The question comes down to how to dream? Often, I forget everything around me was once started as a dream. A person took the courage to imagine something different and bring it to reality. Everything we see, hear and learn started inside someone else's imagination. That's why each of our imaginations matters to the great I AM. The goal is to imagine what you see in Heaven, then trust God to see it through and bring it to reality. Through our imaginations, God wants us to bring His ideas to life.

Imagination is absolutely key and that's why it's crucially important for us as God's sons and daughters to practice using our imaginations more than ever before. Sadly, many of us have struggled to unleash and unlock our imaginations, perhaps due to fear, budget, tradition or other factors. It's time to put those obstacles aside. Think of all the good your imagination can do. What would it look like for parents, students, professors and workers to start imagining the way God has intended? The world would see Jesus's love and imagination in all its glory.

Maybe you want to create a neighborhood of homes in the ocean (maybe orca whales could be their neighbors) or maybe you see a park built up in the sky filled with glass to be able to look down on the world as God does. Maybe you want to create shoes that allow you to bounce to the moon and back? Maybe you can get a person to the other side of the world through underground tunnels in a matter of minutes? God wants us to dream of what we do see in Heaven and bring that to Earth. What do you imagine doing in Heaven?

Our dreams are a gift to love and serve humanity. The imagination sparks key economic development in all people's hearts. It is time to spark the flame. This is why I believe God has brought the message of The Calling before many world leaders and people of influence. He did it so that those influencers could reach out to people of all ages, backgrounds and communities to tap into their God-given potential through their imagination.

Nowhere is the power of imagination more evident than in the light-speed evolution that we've seen over the past few years in technology. A generation ago, the notion that all of us would be walking around with a supercomputer in the palm of our hand would have seemed impossible. And yet, smartphones now seem like ancient technology compared to what's come after them, and what's about to arrive: Artificial Intelligence: AI has already become an integral part of our everyday lives; everything from the products you buy on Amazon to the shows you watch on Netflix are influenced by artificial intelligence. We're now seeing AI being used for all kinds of other purposes, such as making investment decisions for people's portfolios, in lieu of human money managers prone to letting emotions cloud their judgement.

Virtual and Augmented Reality: Goldman Sachs predicts that the virtual and augmented reality industry will hit $80 billion by 2025, a market that would be about ten times larger than it is now. Though AR and VR might often be thought of little more than gadget technologies, the list of potential uses runs a mile long, from construction to data visualization to manufacturing.

Internet of Things: Also known as IoT, this technology refers to the approximately 9 billion devices around the world that are currently connected to the Internet. IoT devices have countless uses, from consumer products such as smart refrigerators to IoT sensors that can be used to vastly improve the efficiency of overtaxed global supply chains.

3D Printing: The number of goods that can be created today by 3D printers boggles the mind. Want to lower your meat intake? You can have your meat-alternative steaks produced by a 3D printer? Want to build affordable housing for the masses? 3D printers can construct an entire house and will eventually be able to do so in mass quantities. By 2025, 3D printers are expected to have an economic impact as high as $550 billion annually. These are just some of the ways which dreaming big has already affected our daily lives—and will only grow in importance in years to come.

Someone's God-given ideas and imagination truly boosts economies around the globe. Allowing the potential to truly dream draws out people's entrepreneurial hearts to thus influence economies. This is the secret sauce to economic success.

WHERE TO START?

First you need to get in the word of God. Hopefully it goes without saying that getting into and staying in the Bible is a pillar to stand on for true awareness and activation of God's heartbeat for the world around us. It is in that mindset and awareness that we can start dreaming and thus living God's dreams. As Psalms 34:7 declares, 'Delight in me and I will give you the desires of your heart.' Our ways and dreams ultimately align with merge with Jesus' wants and beliefs.

Dreaming has impacted the way that we live in so many different ways. Think about the phone that you have next to you, the TV you use for your daily news, the books you read for stronger knowledge, the internet, modern medicine and most everything around you. It was a dream once. It could have been a regular dream or a God dream and when it is it a dream driven by God's word and ideas they impact kingdom history[6]. All of us want to do that, right? It is essential to start right where we are at. The real secret to getting started is to start practicing the use of your imagination more frequently.

In a very sweet film titled "Sunday at Tiffany's," there's a couple who exercised their imagination muscles regularly. They would walk around, see random people and come up with pretend stories of how they came to reality. This brought a sense of child-like wonder and love over both of them. They were also able to dream together. In living life in their way, their hearts' desires were also brought to life. They were able to identify what was truly the dream of their heart. There was freedom to be themselves, fully and completely.

---

[6] *"It doesn't matter how many times you get knocked down. All that matters is you get up one more time than you were knocked down."*—**Roy T. Bennett**

When you begin dreaming, you find yourself imagining what God wants for the world. What does God show you while you imagine a best case scenario for a person, meal, organization etc. That is the place where you are reminded of God's creativity. Isn't that a great place to be in? He calls, we go and the world is changed. Is that not the process that has kept the world going for years? Imagining better is the key to revolutions in all environments, economies and societies. We are on the dawn of a new renaissance for all of God's dreamers.

THE ART OF DREAMING GOD'S DREAMS

Dare to dream God's dreams. Muster the courage to confront your fears and move forward in the face of adversity. Face your fear by taking your focus and attention off of it. Putting your focus and attention on the outcome of God's delivery through you. Before you can discover that courage and live out your calling, you must recognize that the purpose is grander than your biggest fear (Joshua 1:9).

Many times this is what we are called to do: to open up a door we might not otherwise have walked through. We must realize that the angels around us challenge us to make the most out of every opportunity. This could be a career change, a new relationship or even a seemingly mundane decision.

All of these experiences should inspire us to make the dreams in our hearts a reality and know our living God in an even more intimate way.

A fantastic aspect of dreams is knowing God expands and changes them as seasons change. Knowing that our God is on our side explains why once we dream and start living it out, it begins to look different as we press on. It becomes better than we could imagine, but we must trust Him in the process. We are not meant to stop dreaming but to keep pursuing those dreams, no matter what life throws at us.

MADE TO IMAGINE

Our Imaginations and dreams are perfectly interlinked with one another. Our imaginations give our dreams a visual. These visuals help us understand our dreams better and once that is sorted, we know exactly the step that we need to take. It is important to write down things that come to your imagination in your journal, cut out pictures of your dreams and place them on a vision board or wall.

Our imaginations are given to us by God as a massive Heavenly gift to this world to love Him and love His people. If you think about it, we are all made in our God's very image and look at all He created: the birds in the air, the ice on the top of Mount Everest, the volcanoes in Hawaii, the sharks in the oceans, the skin of chameleons, the wings of an eagle and the majestic sizes of giant redwoods.

He created lands at different temperatures, elevations and climates. He created inhospitable terrains such as the Saharan Desert and Antarctica. He also created majestic natural beauty in the form of tall palm trees, evergreen pines and fragrant lilac bushes. God spoke and all of it came to being. My friends, our God created a magnum opus for us to inhabit. When God spoke the world into existence, He created the Heavens, then the Earth and all things in it in six days, before resting on the seventh.

In the beginning, God created the Heavens and the Earth. The Earth was without form and void and darkness was over the face of the deep. And the Spirit of God was hovering over the face of the waters (Genesis 1:1).

Hovering is defined by 'Webster Dictionary' as "remaining poised uncertainly in one place or between two states. Or (of a person) to wait or linger close at hand in a tentative or uncertain manner."

God was waiting for the perfect time to awaken all creation. He was hovering. He was waiting for the perfect time to see His dream come true. Then at the perfect time, He spoke everything into existence. This is who our great God is. He is a mover and a shaker. God loves doing things that we never thought possible. I love too that God created all these things, then He rested.

In His creating of the world, I truly believe He knew this was just the beginning of the most epic tale ever to be told! There was a majestic holy twist to this beloved tale and all creation could tell that they were part of something incredibly special. It wasn't about them. It was about their Maker.

He created a rest day for us each week so that we could celebrate all that He did that week and all that He was about to do. I believe that in

His time of rest, God was using it to imagine all that is possible, to dream inside of His heart of what would bring the most glory and honor to Himself. He was awaiting His perfect timing to create His dream, then He spoke His dream, and it came to reality.

He created:

- The Heavens and the Earth - Night & Day
- Sky and Sea
- Land & Vegetation
- Stars, Sun, & Moon
- Sea creatures, including fish and birds
- Animals and mankind
- Rest Day - I also picture this day to be a celebration day!

And if you think that God doesn't care about the details of how dreams are lived out or what is meant to be, consider this:

"And God said, Let the earth sprout vegetation, plants, yielding seed and fruit trees bearing fruit in which is their seed, each according to its kind on Earth, and it was so" (Genesis 1:12).

God's dreams are meant to happen. As we desire Jesus and worship Him as King of Kings and Savior we need to listen to and hear from the Father's heart. We need to hear what we were destined to do at each time and season. Our God is faithful. He is adventurous, daring and He's the ultimate redeemer[7].

Indeed, such of his qualities are mentioned in what is one of my all-time favorite verses:

"He (Jesus Christ) is the image of the invisible God, the firstborn of all creation. By him, all things were created in Heaven and on Earth, visible and invisible whether thrones or dominions or rulers or authorities - all things were created through him and for him. And he is before all things, and in him, all things hold together. And he is the head of the body, the church. He is the beginning, the firstborn from the dead that in everything, he might be preeminent. For in him all the fullness of God was pleased to dwell and through

---

[7] *"No. Don't give up hope just yet. It's the last thing to go. When you have lost hope, you have lost everything. And when you think all is lost, when all is dire and bleak, there is always hope."*— **Pittacus Lore, I Am Number Four**

him all things whether on Earth or Heaven making peace by the blood of the cross" (Colossians 1:15-20).

As we truly surrender and recognize that Jesus is who we are meant to live for wholeheartedly, we realize and find our true calling and our imaginations become His. Since God is our master creator and designer, He loves dreaming with us every day, in all the small and large details of life.

DREAMING IS APART OF YOUR DNA

When we talk about dreams, it is not just a suggestion but a living, breathing part of every soul's DNA. It is inside of each of us, whether we recognize it or not. The dreams sparked and ignited by God are meant to spur progress worldwide. The dream that you have in your heart, even if it is meant to impact your family, community or nation, should also be big enough to ripple out and touch the world. Let's dive into the glory of God's creation within the Garden of Eden. In Genesis, it was God's creativity that inspired Him to imagine Heaven and Earth[8]. God fashioned humankind to work and rule the land. He spoke and things came to be.

When God spent six days designing and inventing the world, He dreamed up all of the heavens and the Earth, including all the beauty around us—the unfathomable landmasses, the sky, time, all the mammals and all the fish in the sea. God wanted to create a temporary but perfect home for all creation until His final return. He created Earth in the likeness of Heaven. In the very beginning, God created the Garden of Eden as a model for paradise.

In God's dwelling place resides Jesus, His Angels and His saints in an astonishing resemblance of our home here on Earth. In Heaven, we know that anything is possible with God. So why can't this be true here on Earth too? It is written: "..Thy kingdom come; Thy will be done on Earth, as it is in Heaven (Matthew 6:10)."

What if God intended Earth to become even more like Heaven as each of us lives out our Heavenly callings?

---

[8] *Your hardest times often lead to the greatest moments of your life. Keep going. Tough situations build strong people in the end."*—**Roy T. Bennett, <u>The Light in the Heart</u>**

Now, let's specifically return to dreaming within the context of business and innovation. We are born to be entrepreneurs, and America's drive for innovation has been a key to the growth of this nation as well as the wider world. On July 4th, 1776, our Declaration of Independence proclaimed that we are meant to have the rights of life, liberty and pursuit of happiness, with one nation under God. These values have propelled America to the status of a world superpower. All of it was built through the culture of dreaming and innovation. It is essential to understand that these were dreams that didn't just come individually, but came collectively. They were from God because He knew these had to be fulfilled someday. He puts these dreams up for us to pursue and as we do so the ultimate adventure begins.

To further illustrate and see the power of dreaming let's look at many world leaders. Dreaming is what helped Steve Jobs come up with the iPhone and Albert Einstein come up with quantum physics. The Holy Spirit has guided me to determine His dreams for my life in wild circumstances. He led me, with one of my best friends, to meet Billy Graham and it led to the most incredible situation of cleaning the home that Billy shared with his wife, Ruth.

Billy Graham had always been a role model to me, showing me the impact I could have on the world if I followed my calling. So when I traveled to North Carolina, I had a chance to meet him and went to his home. When I got there, I was greeted by one of Billy's caregivers, who told me that Billy was having a tough health day and wouldn't be able to greet any visitors.

I still wanted to show how much Billy's evangelical work meant to me, so I came up with a different way to pay tribute: I offered to clean his home. The caregiver was astonished but, nevertheless, agreed to my offer. So that day, I cleaned the entire house, straightening up cabinets, dusting tables and chairs, and making sure everything was tidy. The whole time I was cleaning, I envisioned all the guests who had come into different rooms and prayed with Billy for the health and well-being of others. I envisioned where Billy read his Bible and where he got on His knees to be filled up. I also imagined where God's dreams for Him started being downloaded perhaps on the kitchen table, the couch nearby or the North Carolina forest outside. And though Billy wasn't feeling up to greeting visitors at first, he had heard about my offer to clean his home. He went above and beyond anyway. He signed a few books for me, one of them being about the love story of Billy and Ruth, which I found particularly special. It was an experience I'll never forget.

FRIENDS

When God gives you a purpose, he also gives you the gift of others to help the dream be fulfilled. Friendship and community is pivotal to living out our God-given purpose.

We often find ourselves questioning what true friendship is. True friendships are priceless treasures. True friendships are supposed to propel you to live out God's dream for your life, not hold you back from it. If your friends continue to hold you back from what God has ordained, you to do or who you're supposed to become make sure to keep your distance. God's true friends for you are going to propel you forward.

Inviting some of my closest friends to be a part of many of these adventures makes the memory extremely special and ultimately overtime blooms and crafts one another's souls to be who God has destined us to be. Be it being present when the Australian Prime Minister was welcoming the youngest girl who sailed around the world with my sister Brittany in Sydney and watching her fulfill her dream to become an RN-BSN nurse and married to the love of her life Lance on a secret island in Hawaii, to producing events at the Governor's Mansion with Michelle and seeing her become an international author and speaker. Then walking around praying and dancing within the White House with Kayla and watching her move to Israel and write and pray for the world. Then, to attending a TD Jakes Red Carpet Movie Event in Dallas with Sharayah and see her become the owner of Colter and CO, author of cookbooks and children's books. To, attending a Children's Ball with Christine and see her walk into her destiny as an incredible children's director and global orphan advocate especially for Ethiopia, to Miss America with Tasha and seeing her fulfill her calling as an incredible global missions director and leader, to then sitting with Third Days Family at Red Rocks with Sarah and see her open up her own remarkable events and floral business, Something Styled, to going to a sold out event with my cousins Mariah and Taylor and seeing them bloom into a nurse at Children's Hospital and sensational communications director, to having help run The Calling's event at Civic Center Park with Leah and watching her produce awe-inspiring Gospel centered events for people to gather and worship, to jumping on a plane with Bethany to be front row at the iHeart Music Festival and watching her live her dream as a children's therapist at Children's Hospital, to watching Mallory all growing up as she was a year older and following in her footsteps and watch her live her dream impacting national societies and communities through events and communication awareness programs. Then to Bre climbing daring Garden of the God's trials and watching her become an annual MC for one the top special needs plays for all America. To Lindsay writing with her grandpa Charlie a new book called Acts, then to Abby playing professional basketball. My cousin Jamie trail the way for couples to love the way God has destined them to. To attending the Country Music Awards with Carrie Underwood and Nicole Kidman, and to encounter Oprah and Quincy Jones at a party celebrating the latter's holistic and philanthropic lifestyle with my fiancé Miles and watching Miles soar into his dreams of creating his second clothing company Christian Combat Gear and leading many important parts of The Calling. The list goes on and on!

All of these experiences were milestones in all our relationships and friendships in meeting world leaders to help one another's dreams plow forward. Experiences build courage to then trust God in the unknown. Now that you know the importance of dreaming with friends, you need to understand how to practice on your own and with others.

PRACTICE DREAMING

As God has continued to lead my heart to spread The Calling's vision for people everywhere to live out their God-given potential He has put me and others in situations for this to happen, but it has come from His divine imagination.

Once, at a Fourth of July event in Washington, D.C., my fiancé, Miles and I were invited to watch performances from the Beach Boys, John Stamos, the Emotions, Pentatonix, Lauren Alaina and more. While watching, we also got invited to the after-party at the Aero Space Museum. While we were there a security guard saw us and said, 'What are you doing out here? Get inside the backstage room now!" She thought Miles and I were Hollywood Celebrities. Ha, we ended up behind the scenes with these legends and were able to spend the rest of the night spreading God's vision of The Calling with them. God wants us to imagine with Him and see His Kingdom on Earth, then go and see it come to be!

The dare above all dares is to believe in Jesus with every fiber of our being. If we do this by faith, our entire world flips upside down – yes, in a great way! Let us look into all the possible ways of how we can put ourselves in a position where you can truly Dream with God. Once you have a dream from God there is no way of stopping it.

Here are some proven steps you can take to put yourself in the right frame of mind to dream:

1. Go somewhere you feel the freedom to write in your journal. Spread out, listen to inspirational music, do whatever you need to do to feel inspired.
2. Mentally let go of everything and leave it at Jesus' feet. This includes all dreams, hopes, ambitions, worries and fears. Fully release all your thoughts
3. Imagine being with Jesus at a kitchen table or on a picnic blanket with you. What do you see, hear, smell, sense?
4. Thank Him for all the blessings He has given you, from the breath in your lungs to the food you eat.
5. Listen for what He has to say or what He may want to show you. Perhaps it is through a family member or a memory. Don't worry if it doesn't make sense. Just listen.
6. Once Jesus talks to you, respond to Him.
7. Ask Him how you can be part of His story this very day.
8. Ask Him about anything that comes to mind.
9. Repeat regularly. Perhaps it begins with five minutes in the morning as you begin to dream. Schedule daily dream dates in your calendar, then gradually plan for longer dream days.

Following these steps, grab a piece of paper so you can begin writing down the dreams in your heart[9]. Dreaming taps into the endless possibilities that are in every situation for each of us and who we are meant to become over time. When you start dreaming, it starts a flame to help others dream too.

For example:

- Mr. / Mrs. _____ has been awarded the Nobel Peace Prize.
- Madam / Mr. President _____ will now dance at the Inaugural Ball.

Some of my most favorite moments and life-changing encounters are when I go on "dream dates" with Jesus. Creating the time to dream of the impossible and asking God for what He wants of me is always fuel my soul.

When entering this process and a dream from the past that hasn't been realized has been blocked or redirected, don't let the pain or sadness keep you from entering into this process of dreaming with God. By continuing to pursue it in the midst of the pain God will not only birth a new dream but, there is healing for you by pressing through.

As you follow through the process, questions may arise: How do you know that you are meant to live out these dreams? How do you know that God has put them on your heart for such a time as this?

The answer to these is found in the scriptures where it is written that:

"Delight yourself in the Lord, and He will give you the desires of your heart" (Psalm 37:4).

We can conclude that as we are delighting in our King Jesus, the dreams and ideas that come to our mind are from Him. How and when, you may ask? The answer is seeking God to bring these dreams alive every day of your life. He will help you take risks, leaps and the stillness, you'll need to see God's full glorious plan come to life. This is why being still with Jesus is so very important. Interweaving our thoughts with His gives us Heaven's Imagination.

"Be still and know that I am God. I will be exalted among all the nations; I will be exalted among all the world" (Psalm 46:10).

---

[9] *"Change course, but don't give up."*—**Roy T. Bennett**

Yes, this happens while we are still. Thus, when we are still, we can listen to God's word and watch Him unfold the mysteries in front of us. He most likely won't give you an exact step-by-step treasure map of exactly where to go, but He will tell you the very next step. In your quest to live out the dream He has placed inside of you, He will instill His divine wisdom into your own heart and mind. You must recognize the dream that God has given you and live it out step by step. Do you want God to choose someone else or do you want to go with God on this adventure? If we start listening to God and start dreaming of what could be, we cannot help but be propelled to live out a dream that is destined just for us.

Persevere until your dream transforms into a reality. Live in such a way that your dream will come to be. Spend time in places where your dream can be inspired. Dress like your dream has already been fulfilled. Talk as if your dreams are already so. God continually compels us to walk by faith, not by sight and we must walk by faith that His plan will be fulfilled.

I know of a special group of people lead by the Bigger's family that spend a special annual dinner casting hope onto each other's dreams acting as if the persons dreams have already come to be. They call is Dream Dinners.

God wants us to imagine with Him and see His Kingdom on Earth, then go and see it come to fruition! He is everything you need and He is your biggest fan. Your dreams and imagination are meant to ripple out and empower families, communities, states and nations. This will empower these entities to their God-given potential. This may even spark economies globally. Our imaginations are a gift to touch each other's hearts.

HOW CAN YOU DETERMINE WHETHER YOUR DREAM IS FROM GOD?

We talked about dreams. We talked about God's dreams. There are all kinds of dreams that we have, with many psychological and scientific explanations that range from our childhood experiences to any recent event or trauma we might have experienced. Either way, it becomes a little difficult for mere mortals like us to understand what dream is coming our way from God and which is the one that is just there as a consequence of our daily lives. I have been there; all of us, have and trust me when I say this, there is nothing to worry about.

Sometimes, you have a goal, dream or plan that seems to be excellent on paper and may even qualify as Holy work (for example, going on a mission trip), but those good works can be your selfish ambitions if you're not careful enough.

"Do nothing from selfish ambition or conceit, but in humility count others more significant than yourselves" (Philippians 2:3).

If you wonder whether your dream is from God or if it is just your idea, then here are five crucial questions you need to ask yourself that can give you proper discernment.

1. HAVE YOU ASKED GOD ABOUT IT?

Before you get caught up in the dream, your best option is to seek God's opinion about it.

When I'm trying to discern the Lord's will, I've found fasting and prayer very helpful. I set some time periods for the fast and prayer. God doesn't want to confuse us; He expects us to seek him first and then listen to His instructions as He shares them with us.

Sometimes the breakthrough of a dream is through fasting as sharing in Daniel 10 when Daniel's prayers weren't being heard so he fasted and Jesus sent Michael the Arch Angel to help him. Make sure to ask God first about the dream and ask for His heavenly backup.

2. HAVE YOU SURRENDERED THE DREAM TO HIM?

It is important to give up your dreams to God. In the event that you don't offer your dreams to God you may transform those ideas into egotistical aspirations or battle to complete those dreams. Remember, when you look for His face to give up your plans to Him, there are times He may request that you abandon those dreams as He has better designs and plans of life for you. When you've given up your dreams to Him, you realize that His ways are best and His timing is perfect, whether He decides to give them back to you or take them from you.

3. IS IT FOR YOUR HONOR OR FOR THE LORD?

While this can be conflicting to answer, you need to take an in-depth look into your heart and be sure your dreams glorify God and not you. It would be best if you humbled yourself enough to honor Him entirely as His servant. He will lift you up at the right time. If you pursue a dream based on your selfish interests, you will lose the opportunity to actualize your vision through him.

This also means you never need to worry about competition. In fact, empowering others in your same sphere of influence will only result in God blessing your calling. Remember your calling is unique to you. You are the only one that can live it out the way God intended. Serve others you know. Trust that God is the one in control of breakthroughs, not you.

4. DOES THE DREAM LACK ORDER?

God never brings chaos or confusion into our lives; instead, He brings clear focus. Hence, if your dream is confusing, it is never from God. He will usually give you a clear vision and mission to fight for. It is our job to walk step by step to see the plan come to be. Remember God cares more about who you are becoming then the end result. Can your character now withhold the dream He wants to give you.

Even when you don't understand it completely, God always communicates the big vision clearly.

5. IS THERE SPIRITUAL WARFARE IN YOUR DREAM?

Even when there is a demonic element in your dream, it isn't a sign that the dream isn't from God. You are most likely being attacked. The enemy will want to put fear in your heart to back away from God. If your dream aligns with God's word it is to be expected that this type of resistance will manifest. The key is not to give up. You can use this as encouragement as the enemy wouldn't fight you if you weren't going to do something magnificent in God's kingdom. God has given you authority in Christ to tear down strongholds and move forward in freedom (2 Corinthians 10:4). Take your position in Christ in confidence. You were born for greatness.

The key is to always pray over your dreams and seek the Holy Spirit to understand them (Mark 11:24). Again, keep in mind that God isn't confused or not ready regarding your circumstances, whether you're contemplating a new dream or staring at the broken pieces of an old dream.

You're precious in God's hands and He is forever ready to lead you into the next chapter of your life, provided you always seek His grace. When He asks you to wait a while, do so, as rest assured, He will reveal your next step to you at the perfect time.

TOOLS TO INSPIRE YOU TO DREAM

The very reason I am writing this book is to inspire you towards The Calling God has for you, this is one tool. One of the most important aspects of your calling remains dreaming regularly. Here are more books and references that might open up your soul to dream. Here's a list of my favorites; hopefully, they can inspire you too!

- *The Call: Finding and Fulfilling the Central Purpose of Your Life* by Os Guinness
- *The Disney Way: Harnessing the Management Secrets of Disney in Your Company* by Bill Capodagli and Lynn Jackson
- *Don't Waste Your Life* by John Piper
- *Activating God's Power* by Michelle Leslie
- *God's Goals* by Michelle Leslie
- *The Circle Maker* by Mark Batterson
- *In a Pit with a Lion on a Snowy Day* by Mark Batterson
- *All In* by Mark Batterson
- *The Purpose-Driven Life by* Rick Warren
- *Believe by* Beth Moore
- *Kays Adventures by* Kayla Ellingsworth Muchnik
- *Wild Goose Chase by* Mark Batterson
- *The Shack by* William P. Young
- *Dream Big by* Bob Goff

The list could go on and on. Dreams are ultimately all about what God shows us He wants for us, our families, communities and world. Dreaming is a huge part of pursuing our callings. Keep on asking yourself, 'What would I do if I knew I could not fail?' #wwydiykycnf

In order to pursue our dreams, it is imperative that we carry the courage to act upon them.

CHAPTER 5

The Superhero Power of Courage

The Superhero Power of Courage!

> Fear not, for I am with you; be not dismayed, for I
> am your God; I will strengthen you, I will help you,
> I will uphold you with my righteous right hand.
>
> —Isaiah 41:10

Before we move on with anything, stop for a second and think. Clear your head and think about all the traits that come into your mind when you think about superheroes. Done? Now that you have thought it through, I can ask you, aren't all of these traits associated with our God, our Creator? They are! The way superheroes can do everything and change everything is through courage. God is in fact the change maker and hero or all our stories. John Wayne once said, 'Courage is not the absence of fear, but being in a fearful situation and moving forward and doing the right thing anyway.'

The ultimate superhero power that we can each possess is courage. The courage to take action at anytime and anyplace to do what God has called us to do to make the most of any situation. Jesus was always living in the moment and that is how He was able to realize when to act. Some might ask how do you know when to act. You know to act when it is something true, right, lovely, admirable, honorable, noble, righteous as said in Philippians 4:8 (ESV). On our way to pursuing our calling we must know that we have to be courageous. Courage when it is seen, courage when being behind the scenes. This is the path that leads us to our calling by living fully in the moment and being Jesus in all situations. This is the ultimate journey.

Even if we know our calling, our dreams, but we don't have the courage to implement them, we will miss out on the adventure of a lifetime. It is important for us to understand and appreciate the wings that courage gives us.

As children, we are encouraged to stretch our imaginations as far as possible and dream the biggest dreams our minds can conjure. Yet, once we reach adulthood that all changes. Society thrusts responsibilities on us; find a job, pay the bills, be practical, be responsible and contribute to the economy. These are the boundaries of adulthood. Dreaming gets knocked as a childish pursuit. Going against the grain and challenging the skeptics who look down upon dreamers, takes an immense amount of determination and perseverance.

But most of all, it takes courage. The Bible speaks of men and women who had the courage to ignore the cynics and keep dreaming as well as inspiring us to keep our dreams alive regardless of the circumstances we find ourselves in. Courage has helped me on my journey as a dreamer and know it is going to help you too.

MEN WALKING IN COURAGE

There are so many examples of men in Christian history who muster the courage to dream big and then implement their dream through courage. It was this courage that led them to achieve all their successes. Through the scripture, we understand and realize that God wants us to be courageous.

There is not one, or two, or three, but hundreds of references within the Bible that support courage as an attribute to have.

First, let us look at direct examples from the scripture in terms of verses, and after that, a few biblical stories to help clear the concept even further.

"Have I not commanded you? Be strong and courageous. Do not be frightened, and do not be dismayed, for the Lord your God is with you wherever you go." - Joshua 1:9

"Then David said to Solomon, his son, "Be strong and courageous and do it. Do not be afraid and do not be dismayed, for the Lord God, even my God is with you. He will not leave you or forsake you until all the work for the service of the house of the Lord is finished."- 1 Chronicle 28:20

"Be strong and courageous. Do not fear or be in dread of them, for it is the Lord your God who goes with you. He will not leave you or forsake you."- Deuteronomy 31:6

Now, let us take a look at particular instances and stories from the Bible that can help us understand the concept of courage. Peter, a simple fisherman, had to have the courage to step out on the water when Jesus asked Him to do so and then trust Jesus to lead the Church through his leadership. It seemed impossible, but Peter took a step of faith anyway. This is why The Calling has water inside its logo. David, a young boy, had to have the courage to use the skill of throwing a stone to defeat a man three times his size and believe that God was faithful to make him king while he was still a shepherd boy. Abraham, an aging servant of the Lord, had to have the faith to believe in God's promise even though he was elderly and his task seemed impossible to have a child.

Courage comes from facing fear directly, seeing the injustices against God's will and stepping up by becoming the hands and feet of Jesus.

If we were all to do this the world would see a whole new awakening of people stepping into their fullest destinies. There is a strong ripple effect that happens when we step forward and live out our true callings.

One person who showed both the faith and courage needed to dream big was Billy Graham. There are many things to be learned from him. Born in North Carolina in 1918, Graham grew up in the segregated South, exposed to all the prejudices that came with that environment. Fighting against racial segregation came at considerable cost in those days, given the societal disapproval or even shunning that could befall anyone who dared speak up.

But that's exactly what Graham did. As a Southern Baptist minister who grew to become one of the country's most prominent Christian evangelists, Graham used his platform and his pulpit to promote an atmosphere that was inclusive to all. As early as 1953, Graham demanded racial integration for all of his revivals and crusades. He even invited the Reverend Martin Luther King Jr. to preach alongside him at a revival in New York City in 1957. More than just being racially inclusive, Graham also welcomed worshippers who were adopting increasingly secular viewpoints as modern society evolved.

More than anything, Graham spent every day preaching to the masses that everyone deserves the right to be forgiven. He also preached that people are saved by Jesus to experience life to the fullest. He would share that God has a special plan for every single one of us and we deserve the right to pursue our dreams. As much as serving God was his dream.

WOMEN WALKING IN COURAGE

The Old and New Testaments show us many examples of women who also demonstrated their courage, dreaming ability and the capacity to actualize their dreams.

Queen Esther, needed the courage to ask the king for the freedom of her family and her Jewish people. She knew that making this request would be against the law and that she could die. But, she did it because she also knew it was the right thing to do. It was a noble cause for her to pursue.

Also, in the Bible, Ruth dared to approach Boaz, even though she knew that wasn't the culturally appropriate thing to do.

Mary, mother of Jesus, needed the courage to believe the Angel Gabriel when he said that she was going to have a son and that the son would be the Savior of the world. The common theme with all of these stories is that every single one of these people saw God's vision behind what was going on and fought for God's side. They believed that by faith they could do it. What does that faith look like for you?

If you act in faith and start moving, I promise you that God will do the rest. Jesus just wants us to trust Him to fill in all the details.

THE RED SEA MIRACLE AT RED ROCKS

As I continue to speak of courage, I must share with you my story of courage as well.

The echo of people singing filled the awe-inspiring Red Rocks Amphitheater. The moment was both thrilling and also terrifying. This was by far the most ambitious venture I'd ever attempted; the biggest dream I'd ever dreamt. Then again, I mustered the courage to come this far. I was confident that incredible things would happen. Maybe even a miracle.

On April 11th I stood next to some of my friends on stage who were musicians like Switchfoot, Chasen, the Pyle family and Lindsay Tucker to complete the Red Sea miracle that we had all just encountered and walked through. While singing, the very glory of that moment dawned on me. It was a dream fulfilled! As it is written in the scriptures,

"Hope deferred makes a heart sick, but a longing fulfilled is a tree of life" (Proverbs 13:12).

You see, it had been years since God had put on my heart that He wanted a future Calling conference to be at this incredible venue at Red Rocks Amphitheater in Morrison, Colorado. God took this dream I had in high school and turned it into a non-profit during my senior year at Colorado Christian University. Pursuing that dream still required me to be bold and courageous, to the point of giving up my initial dream.

I first went to CCU thinking that I would be an elementary teacher because I adore kids. I thought that being a teacher would be the best way to live this out. My Nana was a teacher, my mom was a teacher, so I thought I would be a teacher too. It was then a year and a half into my venture at CCU that God spoke to my heart. He said, *"Chrysandra, you could be a teacher, and you'll love it, but you would always wonder what if."* Thinking what if my vision as a high schooler, The Calling, could become my full-time job? I realized that I didn't want to live with a 'What If' in the back of my mind. What I really wanted to do was to pursue this vision full-time.

Have you ever had a *'What if'* moment?

Don't let it pass you by; it could be the fork in the road that God wants to use to change your life. I know it changed mine!

Now what?

It then sank in for me that all of this was real. I knew in my heart that this is what God wanted me to do. I knew the next step was to talk to my parents about it. They both fully supported me in becoming a teacher because there would be a paying job at the end of it. I knew these conversations were going to be tough. My mom was a teacher, and my dad was an engineer, so asking them to support me in this enterprise seemed entirely polar to my family makeup. My sister was studying to be a nurse. Each of these jobs has very difficult steps to follow, but they also have a path to a full-time career with benefits.

I was requesting that my family support me in a way I would need to pioneer altogether. I shared that I would propose to CCU for my own self-planned major—Business Communications with a minor in Leadership. It was then that my heart understood that my folks could choose not to help me. This could be the end I thought. Yet, I realized I expected to confide in Jesus instead of my feelings of uncertainty. With hesitancy, yet likewise, with confidence and fortitude, both of my folks agreed to help me in the dream I had in my heart.

That was a great miracle. I expected to begin this service at CCU and found genuine involvement by my classmates to join in. At that point, the time had come to begin spreading the message.

The Calling had a large second event at Civic Center Park in downtown Denver and it was open to everyone to attend. We were so honored to have Colorado Senator Lundenburg present at the meeting. At that point, other notables included previous NFL player Bryan Schwartz, the Christian-rock band Everfound, Desperation Band and Jim Copeland and numerous different groups and speakers. We had many philanthropies and organizations on location for individuals to initiate their calling there and afterward, highlighting the Make-A-Wish Foundation. God facilitated this gathering through my peers at CCU and leaders around the community helping me see this dream come to be. Civic Center Park had the highest amount of crime in Colorado at the time, and that is exactly where God wanted it.

We were additionally starting to truly spread the word through workshops and retreats for The Calling. This included IdRaHaJe, Ignite Ministries and many others. The next place God shared on my heart for the conference to be was Red Rocks Amphitheater.

As Student Body President, in high school, I had the humbling honor to speak at graduation and guess where I spoke? You guessed it—Red Rocks Amphitheater. Little did I know, just four years later, I would be speaking there for a dream that God started in my heart: The Calling.

I would often go for sunset runs around my neighborhood and hear God whisper dreams to my heart even at that time. I would look in the clouds and I would notice images. Some of these were of God's hand reaching out to me. Other times I would see a giant amphitheater. I kid you not; I would see the most glorious of amphitheaters in the sky on almost every run I went on. They were magnificent and awe-inspiring.

All day and every day, I would see God affirm the longing He had to have a Christian event at Red Rocks. Due to my Colorado home, I would frequently see Red Rocks Amphitheater from afar. I could hear the heavenly murmur when looking at the amphitheater as this is where He wanted the next Calling gathering to be. I didn't have a clue about how that would happen but knew God could do if He wanted. I didn't realize that there had never been a contemporary Christian concert or conference there. I also didn't realize that I would be the youngest female ever to put an event on at Red Rocks Amphitheater.

All I did know was God wanted me to do it. The next step was to book a date for the Amphitheater and put a down deposit on it. I finally tracked down the correct location to the offices in Denver. I dressed the part and nervously drove to the iconic Denver offices to book an event where the Beatles, Bob Marley, Michael Jackson and others had all performed.

I slowly opened the door and walked in. I noticed a lady sitting behind a glass window at her desk. She glared at me and asked how she could help me. I confided that I would like to speak to someone about booking an event at Red Rocks Amphitheater. She paused, stared up and down at my 20-year-old self and told me to sit over by the wall. As I sat there and looked around, I started to see all the stars who had played music at Red Rocks:

U2, the Beatles and many other timeless musical acts. I began to feel the influence this venue has had on the globe. As I looked around, I heard my name, "Chrysandra?" I turned, stood up, and said, "Yes?"[10]

I shook the gentleman's hand. His name was Steve, and he led me to his office. I walked through the door that read 'General Manager of Denver City Parks.' I took my seat across from Steve and another manager and they asked how they could help. I looked at him and said the same thing I had told the receptionist: I wanted to book an event at Red Rocks Amphitheater.

He looked at me with a massive grin on his face, and he said, "Do you know that this is the world's number-one Amphitheater and the costs are outrageous, even in the concert realm? Who is your headliner?" I replied that it would be Switchfoot and another Christian artist. He then asked how we were going to pay for such an event. "Ticket sales," I responded.

It was then that one giant mountain-sized obstacle after another started to rise from that conversation. I saw all the obstacles rising from pricing to production to weather, yet I knew God was bigger than all the mountains and so kept firm in my resolve. When I asked for the next steps, Steve looked at me, surprised that I wasn't intimidated.

It helped that the other concert producer, Curtis, was a believer (I could tell through his graciousness, his knowledge of Christian artists, and his encouragement). It was confirmed again that there had never been a contemporary Christian concert with speakers, much less a conference. I also learned that Switchfoot had never performed as a Christian band before—meaning they had never headlined for a Christian event due to the nature of their contracts.

On this day, I knew that God was giving my heart peace that He wanted me to pursue Red Rocks Amphitheater to help His children dream again. Even when I didn't have a clue about all the details involved, I believed in Him to complete what He had promised.

What followed was a two-year process of getting everything together for the conference. It was then December 2010, my senior year at Colorado Christian University, we held an advisory board meeting for The Calling.

---

[10] *"You are likely to fall when you stop paddling your bicycle. Such is life. As long as you don't give up, you will never end up failing!"*—**Ayivor, <u>Daily Drive 365</u>**

Everyone there was saying that there was just no way that we could have an event at Red Rocks Amphitheater that following April. We just didn't have enough money. I went home for winter break and I was devastated. I just knew that God wanted to have our next conference at Red Rocks before I graduated the next semester. I wanted it to be part of the legacy I could leave at CCU.

The giants started surrounding me. The deposits, the contracts, the liability, the responsibility, knowing that even concert producers with 40 years of experience do not attempt shows at Red Rocks Amphitheater because of the risks involved[11].

I remember walking through a Walmart doing some Christmas shopping with my mom and sister. I was rolling the cart along when they asked me if I was okay. With tears in my eyes, I told them that I was just so sad. I had spent two years trying to put this event together, and now, all of it just looked hopeless. Tears began to stream down my cheeks and at that point, I didn't care. My heart was broken. I knew that God had put this on my heart for me to do and it just seemed like every single door to move forward slammed shut in my face. The Calling's advisory board was neither being encouraging nor very helpful. I recalled classmates and professors mocking me over the years.

In all of this, my mom and my sister stood by me and reminded me why I was doing this in the first place. I was doing it because of God. I was doing it because He helped me through so much in the past and it was, in fact, His purpose to have the next Calling event at Red Rocks. I promised God and I knew that no matter how many people ridiculed me, I would be faithful to what He had called me to.

Fast forward to New Year's Day. This day was really special because I did really want to lay everything at Jesus's feet and do what only God willed and wanted. I sat at a Starbucks, praying for my dream to come true. It was after that New Year's Day that things started to fall into place.

During the months of planning, I got an email to come and see the campus Pastor and the head counselor. They both sat me down in a room and began to start a conversation that entwined almost every lie that Satan

---

[11] *"Never give up hope. All things are working for your good. One day, you'll look back on everything you've been through and thank God for it."*—**Germany Kent**

would want me to believe. They said: "Chrysandra, you cannot have a conference at Red Rocks Amphitheater. There are way too many risks involved. It cost way too much money."

They implied that Switchfoot would never come on with us as they were a Grammy Award-winning band. They even went on to say that there is no way that Jesus could have told me to have this event; that I was the most stubborn-hearted girl that they had ever met. To end it with a big shebang, they remarked that I was going to have a horrible marriage. I couldn't believe it! It was every lie that Satan would want me to believe about my past, present and future.

By this time, I was in tears. I asked both of them with all my heart, "What if Jesus told you to do something and He confirmed this through years of showing you scripture, clouds, 'God whispers' and personal encounters. I continued, "And what if hardly anyone believed you, but you knew Jesus was calling you to do it? Would you follow Jesus or man?"[12]

He said, "I would follow their wise counsel. I would listen to what they were saying and know that their words were coming from God."

Somehow, that was all I needed to be lifted up. My tears continued, but this time with the thought of how much Jesus loved me. It was the feeling of knowing that God recognizes me and all I was doing. He knew exactly where I was at. I walked out of the dimly lit room and opened the door to the outside. Ah, I couldn't believe what just happened. Did they really just say all those things? The Holy Spirit gently lifted my chin and said, "Chrysandra, they did, but it wasn't them; it was the enemy. I am so proud of you to trust me over man. You need to know that no matter what, you can trust me over any man. I am on your side, and that is all you need!"

My brain became foggy. I was more than just astonished, and everything began to make sense for one second, then in the other, seem unconditionally battered. With nothing in my mind in clarity, I went back to my room, confused and absolutely shocked, as I saw something I had never seen before. Some giants would be coming out and left and right to defeat God's dream for The Calling. I then began to hear from volunteers who had helped put together The Calling that professors were

---

[12] *"Learning to let go is not giving up! It is simply passing the burden to a better fighter, so you can fight another day. (God)"*—**Shannon L. Alder**

telling them that it was a humongous risk for them to be involved and that they should walk away. Volunteers began leaving in multitudes. Then, I heard that advisors who were also professors were told that they could no longer be part of helping The Calling. It was the most bizarre thing. The enemy was on the prowl. The thread that held everything together for me was the peace of the promise that God had written on my heart; that He would fulfill this dream. God wanted a global conference to take place at the world's number-one Amphitheater and no giant or intimidation could get in the way!

After hearing this hard news, I prayed, listened to God and moved on. Then the details all started falling into place. Switchfoot confirmed attendance and the K-LOVE band Chasen signed up. The renowned motivational speaker Rex Crain came on board too. God was able to get K-LOVE radio onboard as well as all the major radio and TV stations on board. Volunteers for the event began to sign up and believed in God's work for The Calling. The news was getting out and ticket sales were coming in. Everything was falling into place!

This is the love and impact of knowing that God is with you. The simple statement goes that one doesn't need to worry when they had God by their side. This is the one simple statement that one can live their entire life by if they wish to. This very thought and belief are also one that instantly instills courage within us. Think about it this way: as a child, when you wanted to cross the road, there was an immense amount of fear and nervousness that loomed upon you, right? However, when either of your parents held your hand while you crossed the road, that fear and nervousness disappeared. This was because you trusted your parents and you knew that as long as they had your hand in theirs, you can take any leap on any road and you will be fine. That is how it works with faith too. Once you have the faith that your God has you covered and that He is there with you, the courage pumps up and the fear tends to die down. Why fear when the most powerful being in the universe has your back, right?

As the event was getting closer and closer, CCU staff would see me and say that they actually heard The Calling on the radio. They were so surprised that details were falling into place. Honestly, I was so humbled in my spirit, too, that God was pulling this historic event together.

Even Lindsay Morton, an artist who believed in The Calling's vision from the very beginning of the ministry came on board. During this time, there were tons of trips made to Civic Center Park and to Red Rocks. This was to remember Jesus' past promises and prophecies for the future ones[13].

It was then, the night before, at Red Rocks, we all gathered and invited the team of volunteers to take a tour of the behind-the-scenes of the Amphitheater. We all prayed and worshipped together that everything would go just as Jesus had imagined! Ah, it was exciting, to say the least!

THE MORNING ARRIVED

I remember all my friends from literally around the world were able to fly in to be part of this miracle. It was an awe-inspiring feat! One dear friend, Christine, even flew in from Brazil to be part of this life-changing event.

The morning arrived. I woke up early and went to my favorite coffee shop. Along the way, Jesus was echoing His love and promises. Spending that fun time with Jesus in the morning carried everything forward. It was finally time to go to Red Rocks Amphitheater. We drove out there and the beauty of it all was all that we wanted to shine Jesus' light like never before.

Evening came, the event was near Jesus was doing something awe-inspiring, and it was such an awe-inspiring, feat to be there. Switchfoot came out, and they were there for sound check. Then Chasen came out, then Zane Black from Dare to Share and the Transform DJs. God was bringing in the best of the best to be part of this life-changing event.

The lines outside of the venue started to grow. The volunteers made every detail perfect from catering, greenroom decorations, to greetings, they were rock stars! The businesses and non-profits began to show up so when people were really inspired to live out their God-given calling at the conference. They could connect with these organizations as mentors and partners to start living out their dreams immediately.

We put our microphones on and were able to start the event. I remember I had run and walked around that Amphitheater so much before the event that I was even able to run around the Amphitheater without a problem, and well, let's just say others were having trouble just walking around. You

---

[13] "Keep Going Your hardest times often lead to the greatest moments of your life. Keep going. Tough situations build strong people in the end."—**Roy T. Bennett, <u>The Light in the Heart</u>**

see, this venue is just outside the mile-high city of Denver - 5,280 miles high and a lot of people came from sea level.

The clock struck 4:30 p.m. and the gates opened! People flooded into the Amphitheater. Transform DJs came out and got the crowd really pumped up. Then, it was my turn to speak. I felt the gentle wind in the air, the calming of the Holy Spirit. It was gorgeous out as the full moon rose above us. God then spoke through my heart and I began welcoming the audience to this awe-inspiring venue at Red Rocks.

I remember conversing and praying to God while I talked. I knew it wasn't me doing the talking; it was Holy Spirit talk through me. I shared how this dream started in my heart when I was a senior in high school. God instilled this dream in my heart to help His people dream again. And I felt so honored and humbled to be on this journey with each of them.

Then, we all prayed together and the night was off. The band continued to play and the speakers began to come up. Rex Crain even said, "This is your moment, Denver, Colorado. God is just looking for someone to say, let your dream come to pass in my life. Let it happen. No matter the cost, no matter the pain, let it happen to me!"

The crowd shouted and cheered. The young and old cheered and worshipped our maker in Heaven. People were rekindled with the magic of the Gospel and were ignited to follow Jesus in the unique dream that He has for each one of His kiddos. It was awe-inspiring with everyone in the audience worshiping God. The Denver Post even recorded that there were more than 7,500 people there who wrote down their dreams and put them on a dream board. The dream boards were brought to the front of the stage. People were challenged to live out their beautiful dreams right then and there by going to the different businesses and non-profits that were present at the event[14].

Lindsay Tucker led the audience in worship and then Switchfoot came out. We were inspired, challenged and compelled to dream and believe bigger than ever before. It was time for us to do the impossible together! Kids were challenged to live out their God-given dreams. Younger adults, grandmas and grandpas were all challenged to live out their calling.

---

[14] *"Never stop dreaming, never stop believing, never give up, never stop trying, and never stop learning."*—**Roy T. Bennett, <u>The Light in the Heart</u>**

Lead singers of Red Rocks conference were singing 'Amazing Grace' at the end of the song; I was overwhelmed with awe and wonder of our great and loving God!

God had performed a 'Red Sea' miracle. In the same way that only God could have parted the Red Sea to save the Israelites from their pursuers, I knew in my heart that only God could have made the seemingly impossible task of hosting The Calling at Red Rocks. Just as Moses prayed for God to part the sea, so too did God act through me to have The Calling's event at Red Rocks become a reality. Many concert producers don't even attempt to hold events at Red Rocks because the planning, logistics and profit potential of the venue depend on a perfect execution. Yet, I felt in my heart that this was precisely where God wanted The Calling to happen and through Him it did indeed happen. All I could do was worship Him!

God had continued to make the impossible possible. I became the youngest person ever to put an event on at Red Rocks. Through His grace and the courage, He instilled in me, we achieved the miraculous.

Everything was made possible because I was confident that, in His message and His calling, He would never let me down. We never know how far we have made it till we make it to the finish line.

As we move on through the course of this book, let us reflect upon ourselves a little. This reflection will help clarify quite a lot.

Here are my questions for you:

- What seems impossible in your life right now?
- What great barrier are you facing right now that seems impossible for you?
- What prayers are you praying for right now, but you've yet to receive results?
- How can you take the next leap of faith?

TAKE A LEAP OF FAITH

Through verses and stories from the Bible and my own first-hand account of my experience, I hope to empower you to know that you can take that courageous step. Understand and know that when you begin walking on the path destined for you by God, you are walking with his hand tightly grasping yours. When He crosses 'the road' with you, everything else arranges itself on its own. The cars stop rushing towards you, the signals are taken care of and there is nothing to worry about. Sure, there might be 'honks' here and there in the form of ridicule or more, but those are 'honks' that need not be worried about because what holds your hand at this crossing is the most powerful of all. No honks can deter Him, and so, no honks should deter us, His children. Beloved children of God![15]

Understand that it is courage that makes you the warrior and hero of the story you are living in to glorify God. Have the courage to do the right thing, and that is, to anticipate your calling and to anticipate the unbreakable bond that you will find with God. There will be turbulences, however, it is only after the turbulences that the plane can land safely, even in the rockiest of mountains, the wettest of runways, and the darkest of paths. Believe big and don't get discouraged. Our God remains the God of the impossible!

Throughout this chapter, we saw examples from within the Bible and also looked at how my life was turned around because I kept the idea and the very application of courage close to my heart. It wasn't impossible for me and I know that it will not be for you either. Take that courageous step and I promise you, you are going to succeed in making your dreams a reality like we discussed in the chapter prior to this one.

May the God for whom nothing is impossible answer your prayers today by taking the first step into the dream He has written on your heart. Let Him write a 'Red Rocks' story in and through you. Let Him take over, and you will be surprised at the miraculous realm that your life becomes. You can do it, all you need is to walkthrough the trials, to the land of the seemingly impossible.

---

[15] *"If you have a dream, don't just sit there. Gather courage to believe that you can succeed and leave no stone unturned to make it a reality."*—**Dr Roopleen**

TO ALL THE DREAMERS 77

Family

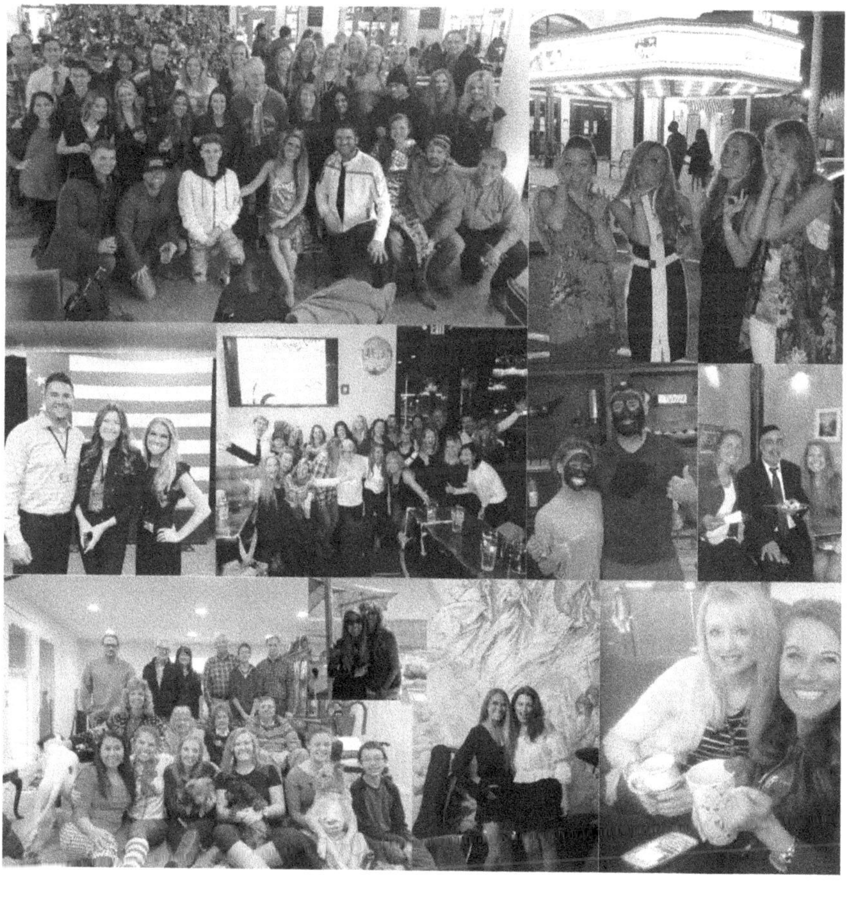

Graduating with my MASTERS in Business, my MBA and Disney Leadership

80 CHRYSANDRA BRITTANY BRUNSON

TO ALL THE DREAMERS 81

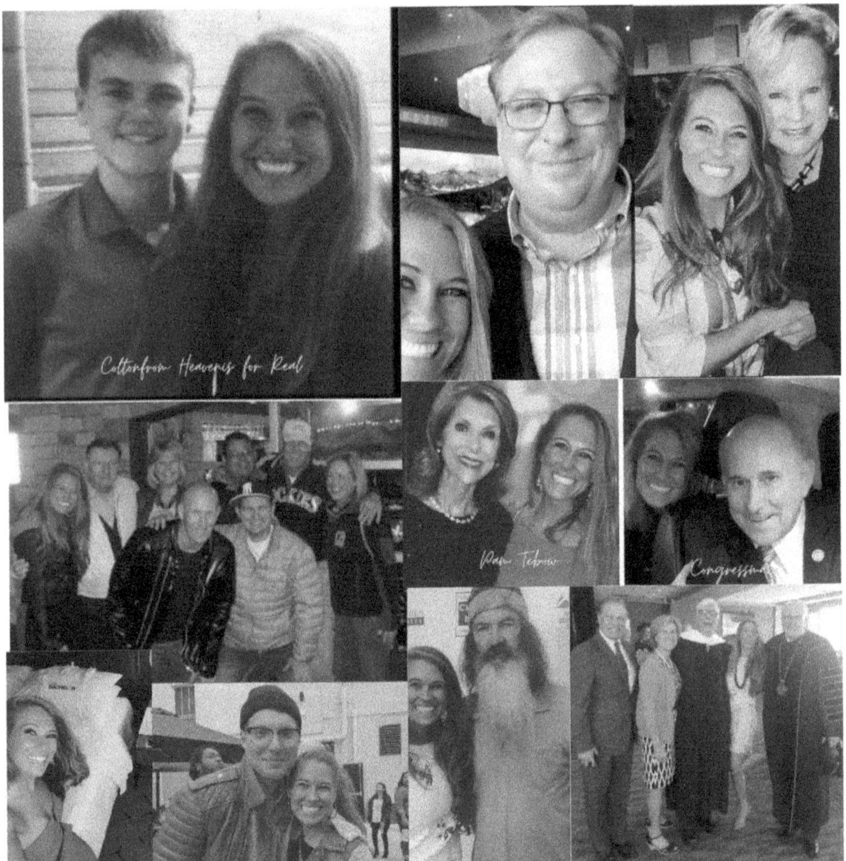

The Calling throughout the Years

84 CHRYSANDRA BRITTANY BRUNSON

TO ALL THE DREAMERS 85

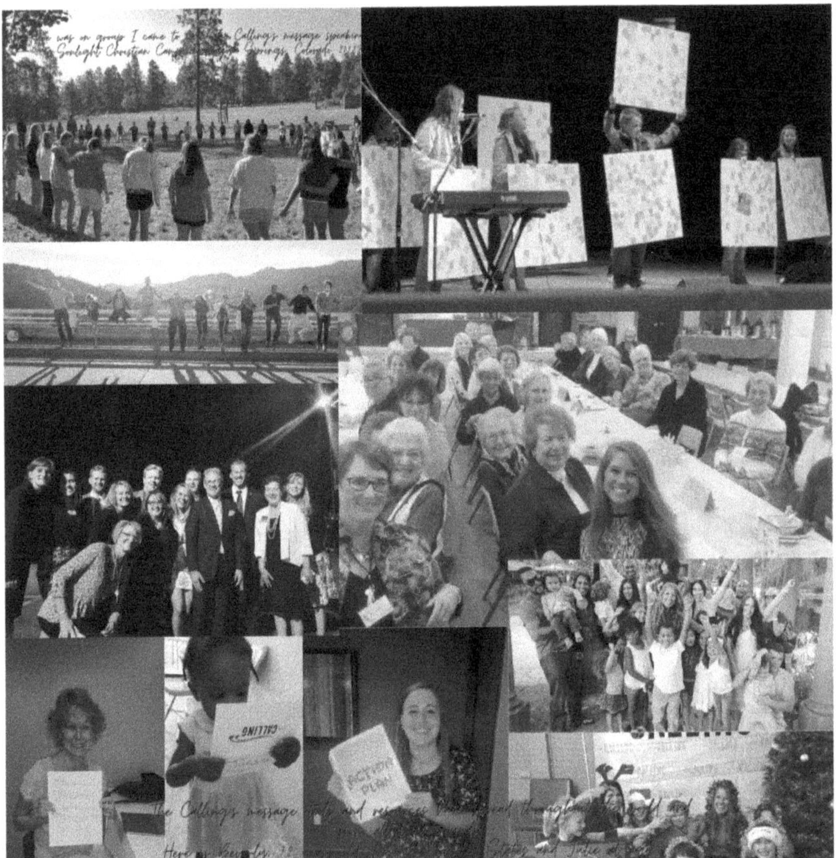

CHAPTER 6
Don't Let Obstacles Stop Your Dreams

When He has tested me, I will come forth as gold!
- Job 23:10

Calling, followed by dreams, followed by the courage to attain those dreams, often then finds those unforeseen obstacles that then make your story become not just ordinary, but epic! Often times the larger the obstacles the bigger purpose God has for you. We should see trials as a compliment not a burden. For God promises to strengthen us throughout these trials and that we will be able to overcome them. Obstacles, define how courageous and committed we are to our God, thus trusting Him with the dreams He has placed on our hearts.

Ah, obstacles. Don't we all hate them? We struggle even thinking about them especially when we are acquainted with them. We try to remove them every chance we get or hurry through them. Sometimes, we convince ourselves that we can't overcome them. The size of the obstacle overtakes the stature of our abilities and we might even stop. The bigger the obstacles the bigger your purpose. We stop trying and we just put a stop to our otherwise undying efforts. Let me tell you something, you are not meant to stop!

Obstacles are only set in your way when it is known that you have the courage, strength and power to go through them. If there is an obstacle that you struggle with, know that God put it there either as a lesson or as just another milestone to be achieved.

AFTER **THE RED SEA MIRACLE AT RED ROCKS**

When God did the miraculous and we had the event at Red Rocks Amphitheater people were talking about the books to come, the next conferences we were going to have globally and the speaking engagements that were going to come. It was all a little scary because it was all going so fast. Everything seemed like it was all coming into place. I was going to be able to have my dream job to be my calling after college. How amazing was that going to be? It looked like I was about to finally travel down the road that Jesus wanted for me with a team of people and finances to support the dream.

I was supposed to fly into the great unknown, into my wildest dreams, instead I was forced to fly back to my nest. It was a treacherous ride, one that tested my ability to keep my hands on the wheel and foot on the gas. The path of God is never without difficulty and problems. The proof lies in Bible, in James 1:2-4,

"Count it all joy, my brothers, when you meet trials of various kinds, for you know that the testing of your faith produces steadfastness. And let steadfastness have its full effect, that you may be perfect and complete, lacking in nothing."

LYME DISEASE, FELONS, AND BETRAYAL, OH MY!

Only three weeks after the large Red Rocks occasion, I graduated from Colorado Christian University with my Business Communications Bachelor's degree, a minor in Leadership and even an emphasis in Biblical Studies. My time at CCU included running Cross Country, leading as a Leadership Ambassador, Leadership Intern, being a part of the Honors society and pioneering The Calling to be a ministry at the University and a 501 (c)3 with the state of Colorado. I was on a mountain top ready to soar.

Sadly, the victory of Red Rocks didn't last long. After graduating, I first went on a CCU excursion to Washington, D.C. meeting many of our nation's leaders with Centennial Institute, former Speaker of the House John Andrews and former US Senator Bill Armstrong. Then I went on a family vacation to California.

When I returned to Colorado I came home to some debilitating and unnerving news. It started with my mom noticing concerns around two men engaged with The Calling. She felt in her heart that the two men were doing something unlawful with The Calling's assets. I had wanted to commit a large part of the money from the Red Rocks conference to different tasks for The Calling, especially for our future gathering in Haiti.

When I came back from California, I went to The Calling's bank to print out all the deposits from The Calling and see exactly where all the proceeds went. My mom came with me to help.

We took a seat at the banker's desk and I asked for printouts of everything. They said my name should of been on another account since this was where a large majority of the money was gone. I was shocked to hear that news for this mysterious account for I was the CEO and Founder.

This is the place where a dramatic movie scene could have been produced. As the agent was printing out the accounting paperwork, he left the work area to get the printouts and my mom looked at me crutching over the desk and asked what was on my elbow. I gazed down and there was an enormous bullseye rash on my elbow. I told her I didn't have the vaguest idea what it was and she said not to touch it. She said that it looked like ringworm. I thought that was pretty gross, however treatable and just continued working through the accounting with the banker.

It was seen through the accounting that money was being shifted into personal accounts without my knowledge nor permission. I was stunned, however, I credited it to a misconception. I was sure that it was a mistake that the other person on the account was shifting money into their own account, surely they would never do that. Right?

While all of this whirled in my mind, we went to Walgreens to get medication for this peculiar rash on my arm. My mom and I were searching for ringworm medication for the bullseye rash on my arm, but we couldn't find any. I went to the pharmacist for assistance and inquired as to whether he could help.

He took a glimpse at the bullseye rash, and he said, "Darling, that isn't ringworm; it looks like Lyme Disease."

The drug specialist disclosed that I should see a specialist immediately. I didn't know what Lyme's Disease was at the time but didn't think too much of it. This was until I did a little research on it and found out that this disease could be debilitating. I did see a doctor right away and the doctor shared that it was a miracle that my mom saw the rash on my elbow. The doctor said I needed to take a medication called Doxycycline right away to fight back the disease.

I learned that the bite of a deer tick could make you get these awful microorganisms that created a sickness called Lyme's Disease. This bacteria can act similarly as a virus and then cancer if not treated promptly. Medication can help, yet on the off-chance that the microorganisms have enough time in your body, they build up a biofilm that is extremely difficult to fight off. The microbes have a tail and that tail will bore through your body tissues and organs before starting to close them down. It first assaults one's joints and causes neurological harm, strength shortages, exhaustion and other huge issues.

My sister Brittany, at that point, returned home from school. She was a nursing understudy who shared that it was so terrible to have Lyme Disease; she said that I could even cause lifelong disability. I started taking my medicine, but my body grew sicker by the day. My joints swelled up, portions of my body felt like a carbonated beverage as my nerves were all being triggered at once and my young twenty something body felt like I was aged. As I was dealing with the symptoms of Lyme's Disease I soon became even more sick, heartsick.

At the same time, my mom put on her investigator cap. She began investigating the two people who were partnering with The Calling at a nonprofit and asked, "Chrysandra, is this the person you were working with?" I answered yes with the deepest heart sorrow one can imagine.

She double-tapped on it, and it was a criminal mugshot! I could barely handle it, one of the people I worked with on the event was a criminal. My mom said, "He is a criminal, a specialist at frauding nonprofits and their leaders. He has been charged multiple times for this kind of violation and he and his partner were responsible for all The Calling's lost money from the Red Rocks event."

It was now that my heart broke. I could deal with there being no money. I could deal with being debilitated with a sluggish disease. However, to be deceived by men I invested extremely valuable energy and put wholehearted trust in - I was officially crushed. The tears gushed down my eyes and all I knew is I needed God's loving peace and presence to hold me.

It was like a movie where the main character is hit every possible way with the most terrible news and the life storm clouds start pouring down.

THE ART OF RESILIENCE

I didn't know how I was going to make it through this mess. I had just graduated from university and The Calling was supposed to be my full-time job. This is what my parents entrusted me to graduate with, and I failed - big time! There were times when I could physically feel the burden upon my shoulders. I was extremely shocked by this whole scenario.

I couldn't believe it. I was ready to fly, but God was instead whisking me back to my nest. God whispered to my heart, "Chrysandra, you can either get upset or you can trust me to walk with you in this valley."

I paused and replied, "Jesus, I trust you, I trust you, I trust you! I don't understand but come help me!" I cried for help. I poured out my heart to Jesus knowing that He was the only one that could fill me, comfort me and help me. Worship music was on continuously, my Bible was open, I was hungry for God to fill my crushed spirit.

Throughout my life, I've come to understand, that *"God is always there to help us, especially when we are at our weakest."* By putting my trust in God, I was confident that He would come to my aid. I held onto Psalm

37:5 promise of committing my way to Jesus and knowing that He will act at the perfect time. I found in this heartache that as I continually submitted to Jesus' will for my life I could find joy knowing that He would use all of it for my good (Romans 8:28). But more than that, I could draw upon my own experiences, the ones that helped me build inner strength, faith and character. Many say the trials and obstacles in life do not get easier but we have the opportunity to get stronger and more resilient. All of the challenges of growing up—emotional, financial and spiritual—fueled my ability to overcome gigantic Mt. Everest obstacles throughout my life.

I have found that resilience is an art. Life allows us to grow in becoming master artists through the heart-aches that we walk through. After years of pursuing God's calling on my life, I've come to understand that there's no force greater than finding one's calling and pursuing it. There is the loving compulsion of hope when you find your true purpose God has put you on this earth for. Think about it. If you're stuck in the middle of the ocean with no person to come and help, you may lose hope, but if you know there is a patch of land in the distance, you have a goal to struggle towards and hope to reach it. You can muster all of your strength and courage and swim for your life. Our calling is that patch of precious land. It's that challenging but reachable internal goal - the one that can save our lives.

Being defrauded, dealing with a potentially life-threatening illness, experiencing financial trouble – none of these challenges deterred me. Not as long as I had Jesus at the center of my life and the echo of my calling He had written on my heart. Look within yourself and you'll find that same source of inspiration, that same calling that will give you the will to press on[16].

RADICAL ACCEPTANCE

Faced with knowing that all The Calling's money that was supposed to go towards Haiti was stolen, I brought the case to a very talented, wise, God-fearing lawyer. He told me we could fight this in court, but we would probably end up the same financially at the end of it. The journey that I

---

[16] *"The world's greatest achievers have been those who have always stayed focussed on their goals and have been consistent in their efforts."*—***Dr Roopleen**, <u>Words to inspire the winner in YOU</u>*

had taken with The Calling as an organization was now under immense turmoil and loss.

The lawyer told me I would be the one that would have to testify the whole time. This meant coming in every day. I would get in trouble and The Calling would face even more risk if I did not. I was so sick with Lyme disease at the time that I didn't know if I could show up at all, let alone daily. I did move forward with the charges, I was told that it would make the news and it would be possible too that it would be paid for.

I found my thoughts tossing and turning like a boat in a storm. What was I to do? My head was spinning and physically my legs shook even as I sat out of nervousness. After praying and asking Jesus to give me only His wisdom, I knew Jesus was calling me to let it go. I would let Him take care of the vengeance. The lawyer created very clear parameters with these two guys that they could not talk about The Calling or with anyone involved in The Calling. As for the rest of it, I would have to lean on the strength I drew from my faith and the radical acceptance that had become a hallmark of my life. Sometimes through all these things, all that you do need is have radical acceptance and faith that God will see it through. Sure, it doesn't always seem to be the right thing to do, especially at the start, but there are, of course, times when you have to simply trust your instincts.

Radical acceptance involves coming to terms with your circumstances, whatever those circumstances may be. It means completely accepting, with every fiber of your being, that there are certain outcomes in life you simply cannot change. Practicing radical acceptance still enables you to feel sadness, anger and any number of other normal (but painful) emotions. It just means that you can feel all of those emotions and still acknowledge that whatever happened was always meant to happen. You can have peace that God is in control.

Radical acceptance doesn't mean giving up. It simply means that rather than dwelling on and suffering over a past event that you can't possibly change, you reframe that event to be a lesson learned. You get to grow stronger from that experience. You get to know God's character more. Rather than regretting what already was, you gain the strength and wisdom to influence circumstances and events that are yet to be.

That summer, The Calling dwindled from being a world-class NGO to a tiny fly on the wall. But I remained determined in spirit and heart. I knew that Jesus was on our side. I knew that nothing was impossible for God and I knew that only through radical acceptance could I rebuild The Calling into something great again. It was time to trust Jesus. I had seen that God created The Calling and I to be His forerunner, His pioneer. Filling that role means going through dirt, pain, weariness, hurt ... but ultimately, absolute wonder![17]

THE PIONEER'S SPIRIT

In these trying times it is often the 'pioneer spirit' that God is wanting to create inside of us. Many people share they want to be the leader of different activities or projects, but how many want the trials that most pioneers need to go through to lead through incredibly hard circumstances. Being a pioneer can mean getting hit with all the blindsides, the scratches, the difficulties, the strife. Truly, for what reason would anybody need any of that?

Over the long haul, I've discovered the response to that question. Indeed, the nicks and scratches hurt a great deal when you initially get them. However, over the long run, they solidify into calluses. Whenever you've encountered and defeated the entirety of a torment and built up that hard shell, you have genuinely caught the pioneer's soul to weather any storm that you may need to go through.

At no point did I grow more calluses than in that one pivotal summer. I went from being a university cross country runner, running 14 miles all at once to scarcely having the option to run for two minutes in a row. I was barely able to move my joints. I even had days where I was unable to walk because my knees hurt so bad.

This ailment appeared like it would be apart of my entire future. The greater test was figuring out how to keep The Calling alive.

As I generally have during my seasons of most noteworthy need, I went to Jesus. For if there's any individual who has at any point epitomized the

---

[17] *"You can dance in the storm. Don't wait for the rain to be over before because it might take too long. You can can do it now. Wherever you are, right now, you can start, right now; this very moment."*—***Israelmore***

pioneer's soul, it is He who laid down His life for our wrongdoings. This verse from Hebrews 2:10-18 says everything:

> 10 It was fitting that God, for whom and through whom all things exist, in bringing many children to glory, should make the pioneer of their salvation perfect through sufferings.
>
> 11 For the one who sanctifies and those who are sanctified all have one Father. For this reason, Jesus is not ashamed to call them brothers and sisters, 12 saying,
>
> "I will proclaim your name to my brothers and sisters,
>
> in the midst of the congregation, I will praise you."
>
> 13 And again,
>
> "I will put my trust in him."
>
> And again,
>
> "Here am I and the children whom God has given me."
>
> 14 Since, therefore, the children share flesh and blood, he himself likewise shared the same things, so that through death he might destroy the one who has the power of death, that is, the devil, 15 and free those who all their lives were held in slavery by the fear of death. 16 For it is clear that he did not come to help angels, but the descendants of Abraham. 17 Therefore, he had to become like his brothers and sisters in every respect so that he might be a merciful and faithful high priest in the service of God, to make a sacrifice of atonement for the sins of the people. 18 Because he himself was tested by what he suffered, he is able to help those who are being tested.

Through His suffering and being constantly tested, Jesus developed the strength and resilience to lead His people and carry out God's will for His life. Indeed, there is no better role model for all of us to turn to when we strive to make the impossible possible[18].

MISS COLORADO & OTHER ADVENTURES THAT LEAD TO MY CALLING

For my part, Jesus began having me do things I had never dreamt I could do. One of those things was becoming a Disney-like character actress and professional mermaid for a company called Wands and Wishes Occasions. It was as if there was a little headquarters of Disney in Colorado and the princesses and pixies could come and visit the community through festivals and private parties. Jesus was so kind to teach me the parallels of these princess characters and their relationship with real life. From Cinderella, Rapunzel, Tinkerbell, Belle and so much more. From the hand waving to the curtsying, I could see that God was preparing my heart for the battles and triumphs to come.

God then opened the door for my body to find creative avenues to start working out again despite having Lyme Disease. Since running was extremely hard on my joints, I learned that dancing could be a great avenue to work out and have a blast. That summer I was at a festival that had a K-LOVE booth. I went in knowing many of the wondrous employees of this great station including the regional manager at the time Jen Lohman.

One of the volunteers was a Denver Broncos cheerleader. Before this point, I had been highly judgmental. I had assumed that there was no way that someone could be a practicing Christian and also be a professional cheerleader.

Yet, one conversation with her was enough to change my entire outlook on the types of people who could be (and are!) Christians. I quickly learned that this woman had an extraordinary heart. Wouldn't you know it she invited me to come to a dancing practice that they were having and I fell in love with the girl's hearts and the workout. This was by far the

---

[18] *"There are five important things for living a successful and fulfilling life: never stop dreaming, never stop believing, never give up, never stop trying, and never stop learning."*—**Roy Bennett**

greatest workout that I had ever been through and I wanted to continue. I was able to learn a lot about their world, the community aspect and the obstacles they have to walk through. While going to many of the Broncos cheerleaders' training sessions (which was a miracle to even know about), I was encouraged to try out for the squad.

The day had come to try out. It was intense, one of the most nerve-wracking days of my life. There were NFL players, Coca-Cola Leaders and other representatives from large corporations presiding as judges. Nonetheless, I did it, and I gave it all I had. You may think it is just a simple little body shake that you have to do. But try performing a 60-second tense song to hit every turn, beat and move with poise and sass while smiling, then you will understand what I had to do. Then you must also be in the best shape of your life, a strong advocate in your community, generous, kind and know everything about football. Yeah, not just what does the quarterback do and how many yards it takes to make a first down. No, I am talking about knowing every position, the intricacies of various plays, which cues demanded which specific cheers and a lot more. These ladies are awe-inspiring!

At the point when the results came in, I found that I didn't make the team. However, the coach approached me and ask if I had ever considered being in Miss Colorado. I said I had never thought about that. She said I would be ideal for it since often the ladies have a nonprofit to fundraise for and advocate during the experience. She said, "Chrysandra, I truly believe you would be a perfect fit!" I replied, "Really, Me?" She further stated that she would give me a young lady's number that was former Miss Colorado. She might have the option to help me and even coach me.

I, at that point, thought about it for two or three days. Afterward, I remembered that my mom was in Mrs. Colorado. How amazing would this be? I asked as to whether this was from God and I heard Him say yes! The goal of Miss Colorado, Miss America was to be the best version of yourself in all areas mentally, physically and active in making the community a better place.

I discovered that this was the only year I could go for Miss Colorado, as I would be aging out at 22. My talent was talking as Belle, dressed in the full gorgeous costume from the notorious Wands and Wishes Occasions, at the event. I discussed inward beauty and that this is what really defines true beauty.

As the event took place I prayed and did my very best. I was humbled as most girls had been preparing for this moment all their lives and I only had two months to prepare. I ended up winning Colorado's Choice for Miss Colorado with Miss America as the people of Colorado picked me! I was very thankful and humbled to be in this sphere of influence. God was teaching me a lot in this season.

A BREAKTHROUGH IN HAITI

Right after the competition and adventure of Miss Colorado, I was booked for speaking on behalf of The Calling at a children's youth camp for a whole week in the Colorado mountains. God took me from glamour to dirt! I love it and love how God does this and stretches us in all these avenues.

I was able to get muddy and wet with the kid's camp at Sonlight Christian Camp. God was training me to love children, inspire them and their families to dream bigger than ever before!

At the same time, God was continuing to let The Calling have exposure here and there at the right timing and with the right influences. Continuing to cast The Calling's vision of all that He wanted to do.

What training have you gone through?

What kind of training do you want to go through to grow into who God has called you to be?

Along the journey of pursuing our God-given calling and dreams, is the essence that most of the time, we have to go through the most horrible of circumstances. Along this journey of putting together our global awakening in Haiti, The Calling and I have faced the most horrible of circumstances. Often, the trials would suddenly hit and they hit hard. These massive trials aren't usually spaced out—they seemed to come in pounding waves trying to destroy all that is in its way.

These tragic weeks often came when The Calling was meant to experience a great breakthrough. During one of these tragic weeks, the most bizarre of circumstances started to occur. This was the week leading up to a massive breakthrough trip to Haiti with those from Google, a world-renown videographer and photographer Annette Biggers and former MLB player and renowned speaker Rex Crain.

The week leading up to my exciting trip to Haiti began with me going to the doctor for a regular visit and I learned that my heart was beating abnormally slow. So, I was put on a heart monitor. In addition to this setback, I also fell and pulled a muscle in a friendly game of kickball. The Calling's donated car was broken into, had my passport was stolen, and a hurricane was heading towards the nation we were about to board a plane for.

At that point, when I got to Haiti, there was another hurricane heading straight towards the nation. We found out that there were criminals within the major church we were working with in Haiti and because of the political unrest I was nearly kidnapped by government authorities. The storm was intensifying and I was flying standby so the airlines almost didn't let me on the flight. This was while I had my knee brace and heart monitor on. I was all by myself. It was a nightmare.

Though, this was the worst case scenario, I knew that this was affirmation that I and The Calling were heading in the right direction. This sense of confidence that came upon me could only be God protecting me through so many life-threatening and physical challenges in such a short period of time. At this point and throughout the whole time, I realized that this implied that we were taking part in Jesus' plans and the enemy was fiercely fighting back.

For ages, Haitians have been the casualties of shady imperialism by oppressor nations, just as defilement inside their administration. 200 years ago the nations president dedicated the nation to Satan and ever since then the nation has been cursed. God is using The Calling and other ministries to take it back and rededicate the land to Jesus. They promote the God-given dreams that are meant to come alive through each Haitian individual. This will then help the Haitians live out their calling's. For if the people of Haiti can live out their calling then others can also have hope in fulfilling their God-given purpose on earth.

In seeking God's heart and what He wants us to fight for on His behalf, we see and hear the injustices going on around us. God emboldens us to stand up to these dangerous forces that often stand in the way of justice. We muster our courage as servants of righteousness, knowing that God is on our side. We must take action.

It was then that God brought a light of breakthrough. Life can be a rollercoaster, but the great thing is that we get to have Jesus buckle us in and be by our side throughout the whole ride of life! Our God is the original pioneer. Even if your ambitions are smaller than His, He can still perform miracles through you. All it takes is the same deep-rooted quality that Jesus possessed: the pioneer's spirit.

WHAT TO DO WHEN YOU DOUBT YOUR CALLING

Our calling will not always make sense to us. Maybe we were not prepared to have it yet, or maybe we don't want to understand it entirely, but it is rather likely that we have certain thoughts. Let's see, have you ever had any of these thoughts?

"I don't understand the reason behind my calling …"
"Why is God asking me to do this?"
"Why would God direct me to this place?"
"If God has called me for this purpose, why aren't things running smoothly?"
"Am I misunderstanding God?"

You have, right? Now, even though there are times we truly misunderstand God or rush ahead of Him, there are also times when He calls us to do what doesn't make sense by our human reasoning. We find out in our journeys that He most often tells us to do something completely outside our comfort zones so we can experience His power flowing through us. Remember our calling is not about us.

If your calling doesn't just make sense, the tips below should guide you on what to do.

Sometimes, God calls us to do something completely outside our comfort zones. There are three top reasons why God can ask you to do something outside your comfort zone. You will also discover proven tips that can guide you through your situation[19].

---

[19] *"You cannot swim for new horizons until you have courage to lose sight of the shore."*—**William Faulkner**

REASON #1: GOD IS HELPING YOU TO GROW AND MATURE IN FAITH

Most of us know this, but we always choose to ignore it because sometimes it is easier to admit that we must go through the hard times.

Our growing seasons mold us to be more like Christ even though they can be filled with frustration, slowness and pain.

If you allow God to grow your character during this time, you'll come out of these times with a stronger faith and a more focused mindset.

Thus, you become ready for the next stage that he has for you.

"…when your faith is tested, your endurance has a chance to grow…" - James 1:3

WHAT YOU SHOULD DO:

- During your growing season, seek God's face to show you aspects of your life which you need to focus on where you need His growth or strength.
- Be conscious of the times when He's trying to work on those areas of your life.
- Be more proactive in seeking opportunities for the Holy Spirit to help you grow in such areas.

REASON #2: GOD WANTS YOU TO HELP SOMEONE ELSE

Sometimes, when you feel you aren't benefiting from your calling's journey, your calling from God at that time might be to encourage someone else (or a group of people) so that you can support, witness, minister or help in their faith.

Keep in mind that God might be using you to improve someone else's life without you realizing it.

"don't look out for your interests only, but take an interest in others as well" - Philippians 2:4

What should you do if you are in a situation of ministering to others, ask him for wisdom on ways to improve your service to them. Seek opportunities to show comfort, kindness and love to others. God is the master story teller. The ability to sow life and wisdom inside someone else most often always comes back to be a blessing to you.

REASON #3: GOD IS WORKING IN SECRET WITHOUT YOUR KNOWLEDGE

God might call you to do something that you do not know the reason for. Ultimately it is about getting to know our Savior and what He had to experience here on earth.

If you're in this situation, you might start doubting, questioning or even trying to give up, but keep holding on to your faith and continuously remind yourself that God is working behind the scenes. Even though you don't see His finger-prints He is still working. God's ways don't always make sense, but they will always give you the best outcome.

GOD IS FILLING A NEED YOU ARE YET TO KNOW.

"Faith shows the reality of what we hope for; it is the evidence of things we cannot see" Hebrews 11:1.

"We live by believing and not by seeing" – 2 Corinthians 5:7.

What you should do if you're in this situation, cry out to God with all your heart and seek wisdom from Him. By sharing your heart with Him (especially your confusion and frustrations) and asking for His knowledge, you can glorify Him better during this season and God promises to help those who are asking for help[20].

"If you need wisdom, ask our generous God, and he will give it to you. He will not rebuke you for asking" – (James 1:5).

There is one common factor among all these reasoning's for God pushing us outside our comfort zones and that factor is obedience.

If you don't focus on your obedience to God who has called you, you will find yourself in a calling that doesn't make sense. You will focus on

---

[20] *"Life shrinks or expands in proportion to one's courage."*—**John Wayne**

the frustrating situation and you'll even spend more time in the struggling season than originally planned by God. God will be faithful to complete His plan in your life, and it can go much more smoothly if we corporate with Him.

Remember:

"We know that God causes everything to work together for the good of those who love God and are called according to his purpose for them." – (Romans 8:28).

If He has called you to something, be assured that he will not leave you or forsake you, He will always be present in every situation till the end. When you choose to obey, you choose to believe and delight in Him. Thus, you'll find your fulfillment in the one who sent you and not the calling itself.

If your calling may seem overwhelming to you now, you can choose to cast your burden onto Him. Be at peace despite the confusion in your journey to complete your calling.

In your pursuit of the mission of your calling, there will be difficulties and there will be many obstacles coming your way. In the midst of all of that, always remember that none of those can ever be powerful enough to break you or your spirit. As long as you have faith in the fact that Jesus is with you at every step of the way you will succeed. Take the first step. He will be there waiting for you to take another.

It is these obstacles that help you become stronger. You will become strong enough that they make you not just step into but also overcome the impossible.

CHAPTER 7

Walk Through The Impossible

"...You are here for such a time as this!"
—ESTHER 4:14

It is normal to all of God's children to be in impossible circumstances. I don't know about you, but I am thrilled that we are not alone. When we recognize that we are meant to be in troubling, horrible, impossible circumstances we find peace and rest that God will come through no matter what. We can even find excitement when we are able to have faith that in these impossible daring circumstances, God's about to work a perfect recipe for a miraculous outcome.

We may not be able to see it, but knowing that we trust God to work everything out for our good as Hebrews 11:6 shares, we must have faith in the unknown to see it come through. In the Bible there are many individuals who trusted God. Daniel had to decide to go into a blazing fire because he would not do what the king told him to do. He trusted that God's will would prevail even if that meant death. Esther stood up to her husband knowing that he could kill her in a second, but she knew she needed to stand up for her Jewish family and community. David knew God didn't want Goliath to triumph and trusted Him to beat the giant with just a stone. Peter trusted Jesus to help him walk on water even though that seemed impossible. Throughout the scriptures one sees the crucial importance of being in the realm of the impossible. The faith of believing and trusting that nothing is impossible for God. We have the faith to see miracles in the world and Heaven on Earth.

Chances are you believe that God can do the impossible, but maybe not for you. If you find it difficult to believe God for the seemingly impossible, as most of us do, it is time to spark the flame of belief once again.

"But Jesus looked at them and said, "With man this is impossible, but with God all things are possible"-Matthew 19:26.

No matter how impossible things may seem, they can be made possible with God's simple touch. We just need faith to trust Him to do it. Whenever I need the courage to achieve something outside the box and way beyond my comfort zone, my first source of inspiration is always looking at Jesus' example. I see that He loved walking through the seemingly impossible in all circumstances in life. This could be Him going where people said not to go, speaking to those deemed as troublemakers, giving hope and a glorious revelation about someone's life, healing someone's body or revealing the wonders of truth of God through parables.

Mr. William Wallace, from the movie Braveheart, provides some iconic internal motivation. In the movie, Wallace, is willing to fight for a cause greater than himself. He found an injustice that caused him to take action. Then, propelled by sheer passion, fierce courage and tenacity, he took action with or without others' help. He trusted God, not man. He didn't want to fight until he knew he couldn't stand for the injustice any longer. When the other army killed his bride in front of the entire village, he knew he couldn't stand back and watch this happen to anyone else, especially to his own community. He encouraged others to see the vision and cause too.

Even when faced with terrible opponents, he always felt comfortable in the land of giants.

This quote from the movie especially fits in this context:

William Wallace: "I see a whole army of my countrymen, here in defiance of tyranny! You have come to fight as free men. And free men you are! What will you do without freedom? Will you fight?"

Young Soldier: "No, we will run and live!"

William Wallace: "Yes! Fight, and you may die. Run, and you will live at least a while. Dying in your bed many years to come, would you be willing to trade all the days from this day to that for one chance - Just one chance to come back here as a young man and tell your enemies that they may take your life, but they will never take our freedom?"

This profound example is for all of us to follow. It is a message that helps us understand that our faith in God. The mere understanding that God stands with us whenever we choose to stand with Him and help us overcome any circumstances brings us courage. It can change the way we behave and react to the world around us. When we are able to look and see what cause we are willing to give up our life for this is when we are able to do the impossible. If we can see Jesus doing it, we can do it. Remember God leading us to the land of giants is normal to him so that He receives all the credit for defeating them. Although every story doesn't always end up in a victory at the end of one's life. Even though William Wallace was beheaded for following his calling in his fight for freedom of the Scottish nation, God rippled out Wallace's legacy to touch others hearts that then lead to his nation's freedom. We can't always judge a defeat or victory. Only God can be the referee but when we are living for Him in the 'Land of Impossibility' He will always ripple it out to be a part of His grander larger epic story He is creating. God will accomplish His will no matter what, we just have a chance to be part of life right now!

WHAT CAUSE ARE YOU WILLING TO GIVE UP YOUR LIFE FOR?

We must look for a cause that we believe in with all our hearts, this is where God is able to open the doors and see the miracles we read about throughout the Bible. Steve Jobs once said: "Your work is going to fill a large part of your life, and the only way to be truly satisfied is to do what you believe is great work. And the only way to do great work is to love what you do. If you haven't found it yet, keep looking. Don't settle. As with all matters of the heart, you'll know when you find it. Have the courage to follow your heart and intuition. They somehow know what you truly want to become."

If the man who founded a billion-dollar enterprise is saying this, it is going to have some weight to it, right? All of us need to fight our own battles and sometimes we hesitate to really do work that we believe in. A lot of times, this hesitation comes from a lack of courage – one that goes missing from within us as we get deeper and deeper into what the societal pressure requires of us. However, the fact remains that for anyone to find their true calling, they need to know the cause they are living for is bigger than themselves.

It's finding that courage and the action that follows—especially when the stakes are at their highest and our challenges seem the most daunting—that helps us find our true calling. God is all-knowing and holds all the answers and desires of our hearts. He blends those desires of our hearts when we have faith in Him to then rally and dare to help a situation we see with Heaven's touch on it. It could be an orphanage that we want to help. It may be a business we want to start and pour the profit into a nonprofit. It may be running for office to be a spokesperson for the public on behalf of these issues.

When we tap into His creative nature, we can aspire to live out the stories that Heaven will remember for eternity. Remember we have all of Heaven cheering for us. Do not give up. I want my story to be one of adventure, great love, triumphs and awe! What kind of story will people tell of your life? The answer to this question is within you. The way that you are remembered here on earth totally depends on who you are and all the battles that you have fought throughout the course of your life. These battles define you. The end result of these battles might not have an impact on how you are remembered, but you will be remembered more so on how you took on those battles. It will be the courage that you displayed that the world will remember. What story do you want the world to remember of you? This story will also be one that Heaven will replay. Don't be afraid to do the seemingly impossible.

It is when were in circumstance that we think we are drowning that Jesus does the miraculous!

FINDING COURAGE AND STRENGTH IN HAITI

"Finally, be strong in the Lord and in the strength of his might. Put on the whole Armor of God, that you may be able to stand against the schemes of the devil. For we do not wrestle against flesh and blood, but against the rulers, against the authorities, against the cosmic powers over this present darkness, against the spiritual forces of evil in the heavenly places. Therefore, take up the whole Armor of God, that you may be able to withstand in the evil day, and having done all, to stand firm. Stand therefore, having fastened on the belt of truth, and having put on the breastplate of righteousness ..." Ephesians 6:10-18.

During my long-anticipated (second) visit to Haiti, I sat down in a music studio, listening to government officials and a pastor who were all speaking in Creole. They discussed a topic obviously of great importance, as was indicated by their great expressions and passion in their responses. As I sat there, listening to the buzzing flies, powerful voices and the Pastor's music, I remembered the night before.

The night before, I was attempting to hop in the cold shower to clean off from a day of serving in the beloved Haitian orphanages. It was an exhausting yet fulfilling experience and where my mind and body a great night's sleep. However, the modest goal of a quick, frigid shower to clean up before sleep proved to be too much to ask. None of the showers were working and there were tarantulas lurking around. The shower walls were behind the Voodoo Camp next to where I was sleeping, were beating in the background as they were doing their nightly Voodoo Worship. At the same time, the shower water wouldn't turn on for me in my stall, but then one shower five rows down started to turn on all by itself. I could feel the spiritual warfare arise in the atmosphere and I had goosebumps from head to toe. I decided to run to my room. With no shower, I went to my bed and remembered that it was Valentine's Day. The day of love celebrated all over the world! I thought to myself, *"What a great Valentine's day - full of spiritual warfare, alone, with nothing to show for the vision that You have given me, Jesus."*

The whole trip had been incredibly discouraging given my lofty goal: To find a possible venue, sponsors and leaders in Haiti for our next big event for The Calling. Yet, a part of me remained adamant God would succeed. Our previous conference before had been held at Red Rocks, bringing together Grammy Award-winning entertainment and thousands of guests. I knew that if God could do that, He could do anything. Yes, anything, even put on a million person global conference in the poorest country in the world to help the people of Haiti live out their unique purpose. This was God's vision He put on my heart. I tried to focus on putting my faith and trust in God and He would take care of the rest.

Still, while I had those aspirations, at the moment, I was genuinely exhausted and feeling hopeless. Then, I saw a copy of the Bible in my room; I flipped it open and it turned to a passage about God always giving us our heart's desires (**Psalm 37**). I chuckled inside, thinking this was far from my heart's desire. Just then, the Holy Spirit spoke to my heart like never before: "Chrysandra, Happy Valentine's Day! Do you love my Valentine's gift to you?"

I didn't know what the Holy Spirit was talking about until I heard Him say, "My gift of bringing you down to Haiti!" I was jolted. My heart was beating faster than I could have imagined. My hands and feet were shaking nervously as I understood God's plan.

It dawned on me: I had spent years praying and speaking God's promise and I was finally in Haiti, where God had urged me to come for a long time. I was amazed at God and His greatness. In thought, I said to Him, *Jesus, you are so sweet! Thank you so much for having me here for Your great purposes. Do what only You can do!* It was then that I fully surrendered by knowing that if God wanted me to be in Haiti and have The Calling's next global conference there, then He would provide everything in His time. He would bring all the right people and I would share the vision of The Calling at the perfect time. This was the best Valentine's gift!

I remembered all of this from the night before and then suddenly the pastors and leaders stopped speaking in Creole and turned to me and said, *"Chrysandra, tell them the vision God put on your heart for Haiti."*

I knew God had intended for me to tell them. So, I did. I shared with them what God had put on my heart. Then, the Mayor of Leogane (a governor in Haiti) looked at me and asked, *"Chrysandra, do you want to go to the church service?"* She went on to say that it was an all-night church service. I told her that I would love to. I thought how amazing it would be to witness a few hundred devout Haitians worshiping King Jesus.

And so, she and all the leaders that were in that room started to walk towards a gorgeous hilltop. The Governor took my hand, as it is a sign of great warmth and gratitude. We got to the top of the hill; then I looked down and saw thousands of people! I was in total astonishment. A holy awe came upon me.

We started walking down the steps towards the front. I thought it was such a blessing to walk down and be towards the front. I listened to the passion emanating from these beautiful hearts - young and old. Many kids were jumping with praise, clapping with joy and the elderly were doing the same. I realized their true only hope and strength was Jesus Christ Himself. Good Lord, what a sight it was! Many of these people hadn't eaten in days and didn't know how they would survive the next day, but yet they were, living in the moment for God. They praised their Heavenly Father for the provision He was giving them in their present and thanking Him for eternal salvation.

While all of this was soaking in my soul, the Mayor said that over 40,000 people were worshipping Jesus that evening. I couldn't believe it. It was the closest thing to Heaven that I had ever witnessed.

Afterward, we walked past the front row and directly to the stage. I couldn't believe it. There were only a few seats on stage and one of them was for me! I saw the Governor, dressed entirely in white, go to the stage and fall on her face before King Jesus. She laid on the floor, worshipping Him, surrendering herself to His glory. She was a real example of a Queen. She walked with great authority and confidence and then bowed and worshipped Jesus like I have never seen before. 'Ah, Holy Christ, you are the sweetest and most glorious storyteller,' I thought.

Then they called forth the demon-possessed to pray over them. It was something I had never encountered before. More than three dozen people came forward. The sight was unfathomable. Many of them were in rags, rolling on the ground, foaming at the mouth, raging demonic shouts. My mind refused to process what was unfolding in front of me. I had never seen such a thing. Someone asked if I wanted to leave. I replied that this was very good for me to see. This was talked about throughout the Bible and now I would get to see first-hand what He was trying to explain. People came and prayed over them and God healed many of them in His name.

The Pastor then calmed the sea of more than 40,000 people on the hillside and began to give announcements. He then gave me a gesture to go up to the microphone and introduce myself. I did that, inhaled a deep breath, and thought, *"Okay, Chrysandra; you can do this. Your name is super long, but you have been practicing since you were two years old. You can do this!"*

I was handed the microphone and I introduced myself, telling my name and that I was from Colorado. A gentleman translated it and gave it back to me. It then dawned on me that they wanted me to speak. I thought, *God, what do you want me to say?* I wasn't prepared for this. It is then that the Holy Spirit spoke to my heart and said, *"Chrysandra, tell them what I have told you. I will speak through you right now about what to say."*

Through me, the Holy Spirit spoke God's powerful vision over the people of Haiti. He said that God has not forgotten about Haiti's beloved nation and that God wanted to rededicate the whole country to Himself. God wanted to help each individual live out the God-given dream that He had desired for them and spur on entrepreneurship in the land. Thus, He would then transform what is economically the most impoverished country in the world into a world superpower. Consequently, He would show that if Haitians can dream God's dreams again, then no one in the whole world has an excuse. Then I ended by sharing that nothing is impossible for our God and the best is yet to come!

As I concluded speaking, that audience of 40,000 stood up and shouted, "HALLLLLLLLLELUJAH!", with all their arms raised in the air! The feeling was almost unreal. It made my heart glow with happiness, as my face reflected just a little percentage of what I was feeling. My smile went from one ear to the other, as my jaw almost hurt from smiling as hard as I was.

I stood there watching people worship their hearts out. Their shouts of faith warmed my heart and soul up in a way like never before. Jesus was King and He did what only He could do. I had no idea who these people were, what the church was, etc. I eventually found out that this church "happened to be" the largest one in all of Haiti. God loves a good setup. Each aspect of our lives is meant to be an epic movie. God has taught me that life is often like movie scenes. All of our stories are connected and extraordinary and we have the master storyteller writing our stories if we fully let Him! He whispered to my heart, *"Chrysandra, nothing is impossible with me. You can do all things in my Holy and Righteous name! What I promise I will fulfill - no matter how impossible it may sound or be!"*

Through the experience, it dawned on me that God is the master storyteller. He uses every part of our stories to weave together His greatness and holiness. In my case, God presented giant obstacles for me to overcome during my time in Haiti. The outcome wasn't one of fear or despair. It was an opportunity to speak in front of 40,000 of God's children, people entirely committed to embracing the word of God. What felt like an impossible task to achieve became a possibility before I would even know it. Impossible can be made possible; the only difference between the two is faith.

Remember and know, nothing is impossible with our great God! He will fulfill your heart's desires in the hardest of circumstances. Step out of your comfort zone to the land He is calling you to and have faith He will slay the giants through you one step of faith at a time. Don't back down, claim His truth over the situation you're in, even right now. Know you are not alone. You have all of Heaven's Angels and loved ones cheering you on and they have gone before you. Imagine what they are saying to you now:

Keep Going!
Don't give up!
Trust Jesus with all your heart!
Live everyday as if it were your last.
Use the resources you have to slay the giants in front of you
Live in such a way you want to be remembered for all eternity
You were born to do great things.
There is no one in all creation like you.
We are all cheering you on, you can do it!
Stand up for the injustices you see in the world!
Make the most out of every circumstance!

You were born to be the hero of the impossible circumstances you will face when living out your calling. You can do it, remember all of God's children go through this. You were born to be the hero in your story.

CHAPTER 8
Romantic Relationships

"In the end, it's not the years in your life that count. It's the life in your years."
—ABRAHAM LINCOLN

Would you say that God is a hopeless romantic and the perfect storyteller? My sweet friends, He is! God absolutely loves love stories. Let's recall the stories of Adam and Eve, Boaz and Ruth, Joseph and Mary, Esther and King Xerxes and His love story with you and me! God shows us how to love astonishingly well. He shows us that adventure, battles, hopes and dreams are essential to any good love story. Just as God *loves* love, we are made to love too.

GOD HELPS US UNFOLD OUR OWN LOVE STORY

As I was writing this chapter I walked into one of my most favorite hidden enchanted libraries in a fairy tale hotel in the mountains of Colorado. When asked about what people would want to read about in this book about calling and purpose, a surprising amount of people shared they would love to learn about love and relationships. Thus the inspiration was sparked. As I sat down to eavesdrop on a conversation between two wonderful women. These women, in their 80's with their hair greyed to perfection, voices mellowed and wrinkles glowing beautifully, with their blush set on their smiling cheeks, started talking to each other about their romances. It reminded me of Randy Travis' song, 'Forever and Ever Amen!' There is a lyric in the song that says, 'I am going to love for as long as old women talk about about old men!'

Ha, one of these gorgeous grandmas talked about how head-over-heels she and her husband were with each other, how her husband would look at her on a crowded escalator and say at the top of his lungs that he just wanted to give her a big kiss. "We love just looking at each other!" she beamed.

The grandma went on to say that they had been together for 60 years. This kind of love is not by accident. It is the real deal. God wants to confirm that His fairy tale love is alive and well. Call me old-fashioned or a dreamer, but I do truly believe in story-book, Heavenly love. We need this kind of fiery passion for pursuing our own individual callings. This is the passion that adds to our relationships. Our desire for relationships, yes the fire and passion that we find in love with each other and our surroundings are part of God's plan. It is His eternal love that helps us find love within this world. He is the ultimate romantic storyteller.

Mickey and Minnie, Romeo and Juliet, Cleopatra and Mark Antony, and Heathcliff and Catherine are all fictional love stories written by some brilliant writers, but all of us are created to yearn for a love story for ourselves. If mere mortals, as writers, can write brilliant love stories like that, imagine the kind of romantic storytelling the God can do.

If God didn't reveal to us who we were supposed to be with, we would probably end with a hard marriage, maybe mediocre or even good, but not great. Who wants that though? Don't we all want to marry our soulmate and have a legendary love story! Why settle for ok, when God wants to have an epic marriage.

God doesn't just leave it up to chance to marry whoever we think is cute, has a kind family and a good job. Yes, we have free will to marry whoever we want, but the beautiful challenge is believing that God cares enough and loves each of us enough to guide us to the best mate and teammate we can possibly find.

God loves each of us so much. He knows that it is way too much to simply leave our love story to chance. We are talking about the one we are meant to unite with in every way—in body, mind and spirit. Think about the alternative: Are we supposed to think that we can just be with anyone we think might be pretty good for us? God allows us to form a covenant relationship and then He confirms our destiny and vision with Him. Along the way of pursuing Jesus in that dream and calling comes the beauty of being united with our soul mate.

I believe that in our walk with God, we learn that the tune of our conscience is filled with the Holy Spirit. He tells us what is of Him and what is not. He gives our spirits a yes and no. He helps us unfold our own love story – indeed, the best story ever told through each of us!

It is vital for our hearts and our souls to be sure that we know our God cherishes every one of us to such an extent where He realizes that it is an excessive chance to just leave our love to risk. Consider the other option: are we expected to believe that we can simply be with anybody we think may be seemingly amazing? God permits us to shape a contract relationship; at that point, He affirms our calling and mission in life and will give us someone to help fulfill it. Along the way of seeking after Jesus in that relationship comes the excitement to be joined with our perfect partner.

God has made us to yearn for love and that starts with Him. Well, and I am not saying this because I need to say this for my book or it is just something that I have read or been told. It is something that I have personally experienced. And as I have stated throughout the course of this book, I would like to inspire your hearts with my personal story here as well.

MY PERSONAL STORY

I waited 29 years to have my first boyfriend and now fiancé Robert Daniel Miles Bradshaw. Yes, I had gone on dates with guys and met amazing guys with lots of different backgrounds. They had good hearts but I just knew I didn't meet the right one yet. I had been close to those very words of boyfriend and girlfriend coming out of my lips. But God had me wait for a very long time to go on this venture. I am so glad He protected me for the one He had for me. I'm happy to say that my patience paid off. I am now with a man beyond my wildest dreams.

God knew exactly what heart desires to fulfill when we met each other. We found Jesus in one another and an unconditional love. I am so thankful God had me wait for Miles. It was very surprising though because he knew my family on my mom and dad's side. Before deciding whether or not to meet Miles I was at a charity event at Children's Hospital dressed as Wonder Woman, and randomly ran into my cousin Jenna. I saw her from afar and in my costume I took her and said Jenna it's me, 'Chrysandra!' We both laughed as it was hilarious I was dressed up. But I looked her in the eyes and asked her opinion of this mystery man Miles and if I should go on a date with him aka coffee. She said laughing 'I would try it out Wonder Woman!'

Well Miles continued to reach out to me and I started to get to know the sweetest soul I had ever known. I could tell he had a golden spirit filled with God's love and I found out that he even loved Frank Sinatra, one of my all-time favorites. He loved and believed in The Calling and he had requested to get together and know more about The Calling and I. I said no about 20 plus times because honestly I didn't know who he was and I wasn't in a hurry to go on a date. Ha, I had heard the line 'I would like to go to coffee and get to know more about The Calling, a lot!' Some girls get, 'Wow girl where are your wings, I mean you're an angel,' and I got The coffee and The Calling pick up line.

Miles did not give up on me and I felt adored and pursued. I was able to get to know his Heavenly golden heart in text messages and phone calls as he would say he wanted to see how I was doing. Deep down inside I knew that if I were to meet Miles that my heart would be his.

Both sides of my family had heard about this 'Miles guy' and said I should for sure meet him for coffee. My mom even said Chrysandra, 'If you don't give this guy a chance I give up!' Ha, this did propel me to write Miles on Christmas and tell him I had a Christmas present and would meet him for coffee the next day. I knew if I said a few days later I would probably chicken out as this was scary territory for me to be in, the land of the possible Man. Done, done, done!

Well, the next day came and Miles showed up early to the coffee shop and as he stood up my heart melted and truly felt like it was love at first sight. I couldn't believe that the most handsome guy I had ever seen was 'Miles!' He says that it was love at first sight for him too. There was a magical Heavenly spark right away. His heart to fight for the least of these in the world, generosity, courageousness, entrepreneurism, love for The Calling and Christ-likeness won me over.

This man wrote me the most amazing love letters, gave me a multitude of surprises and most importantly fought for the dreams God had put in my heart. Now over four years later we are engaged and thrilled to live out God's calling for our lives together as one as Husband and Wife.

We didn't know that we would have to go through such heart breaking trials of death, fires, and much more. These tragedies were either were going to lead us closer together or apart. We now look back being thankful that we could be in each other's lives through this tragic season.

Life is full of ups and downs but when you have your best friend and soulmate by your side to weather the storm with you, you have a peace, comfort and supernatural strength to walk through it and become stronger and more like Jesus on the other side.

WHEN IT WASN'T WORKING OUT

I remember though that when past relationships were not working out, I would often be frustrated about the waiting process.

Due to my mom and dad splitting up have made the topic of marriage an even more special one for me. It is the deepest desire of my heart to be united with my beloved that God had ordained for me from the beginning of time. Likewise, I enjoy giving others hope of finding all that is possible when it comes to love. I believe that it is rare to find a couple that actually awaited God's best for them. His best plan doesn't necessarily mean it's going to be easy. But it will mean that God's peace will be a pillar for the relationship to last through any and all fires.

In fact, I remember Brittany and I being very little and asking our Daddy what he was looking for in a future mate. We were asking because he was our absolute superhero and he had found our mom. He said someone who was kind, sweet and always gracious, who said their 'pleases and thank you's.' Doesn't every girl think that way? They watch their father be the most amazing figure in their life and they often want to marry a man that carry many of the same values and characteristics.

Well, from that moment on, Brittany and I would always say please and thank you. If one of us didn't say a please or thank you, we would nudge one another to say it.

We asked what drew him to fall in love with our mom and he shared that she was kind, gracious, adventurous, fun, smart and so much more. It was from that moment on that we wanted to be like that too. We wanted to marry someone like our Daddy and be like our Mommy. Our inspirations began at home with our parents and then those inspirations went further for us in many media outlets.

INSPIRED BY UP, BRAVEHEART AND THE NOTEBOOK

Three of my favorite movies of all time are *Up*, *Braveheart* and *The Notebook*. All of them contain love stories that never stop inspiring me. Though each of these love stories includes many wonderful elements, I like to focus on the three P's of relationships in these three films.

THE PLAYFULNESS IN *UP*

One of my favorite love stories comes from the Pixar film, *Up*. For those who haven't watched this life-changing movie, one can be encouraged in the very first few minutes by watching a young boy, Mr. Fredrickson, stumble upon Ellie.

Ellie was a wild adventurer. Their adventure starts with little

Fredrickson seeing that little Ellie needed help getting her lost balloon. This is a hint for all you guys out there: If you see a girl you like, look for ways to help her, love her and humbly serve her. They lived life to the fullest together. They made the most of every situation, pretending that when jumping over a crack in the cement they were actually jumping over the Grand Canyon and climbing over a tree stump that was meant to be Mount Everest.

They dreamed together and loved each other through the hardest of life's sorrows. It is important to be able to play with your soulmate. It is important to dream together, create together and build together. In the first few minutes of the movie one sees how quickly life goes by. It's a reminder to make the most of every day, especially with your future bride or groom.

THE PURSUIT IN *BRAVEHEART*

William Wallace passionately loved life. He fought for everything that was righteous and good.

As a boy William recognized God's kindness, as God pointed out his future true love. The simplicity of childhood love brought great admiration on both sides, leading to a more meaningful bond in adulthood. In one of the hardest times of William's life, this little girl comforted him. She brought him a flower, a sign of great endearment.

William carried this flower with him for more than 20 years. When he was ready to pursue his bride-to-be, he gave the flower back to her. He wooed her by first trying to beat a giant man in a throwing contest, then horseback rides, dances in the rain and much more. He carried strength in his every move towards her. He would watch her from afar in admiration. Watch for little details. He knew that pursuing wasn't just about a physical posture of walking over and talking to a lady. His heart and soul recognized that it was about watching, admiring her beauty, chasing after this heart's desire in the daily details. He knew that he was meant to spend eternity with her. He fought for her heart and won her in marriage.

It is after great moments of love in marriage that he lost her to death by criminals. This is where William saw his bigger purpose, to fight for the freedom of his country and fight on behalf of his late bride.

Many times pursuing something or someone requires a period of waiting. It costs the soul to rest in God's faithfulness and not one's own strength. The novels *Wild at Heart* and *Captivating* by John and Stasi Eldredge are both stories of the great roles we take on to live out the dance of romance.

Romance is birthed from the heartbeat of God. Most of the time it requires us to wait on the Lord. The waiting period in any relationship reflects the waiting and patience of Christ himself. It is important to recall the first attribute of love in 1 Corinthians is "Love is Kind." William could have thrown away his hope to anyone else, but he waited to come back to his first love. That wait grew the love and respect in the woman's heart. This respect allowed her to know that she could soulfully trust Jesus' purposes no matter what.

The girl also had to choose to wait on him as well. She could have married any other man, for she was very beautiful, kind and courageous. She had to have the courage to wait for her true love to pursue her with a heavenly love. She trusted that a love would come and take her breath away. She delighted in the role God created for her, and continued to anticipate her love. She knew deep down that her true love would come back.

I imagine her waiting for William throughout the decades, walking through the very flower gardens where she picked the flower that she gave to him. I see her going to the top of hills and watching from afar to see if he would come then.

Though waiting for your perfect partner can be painful, it can also bring out our heart's great joy, knowing that we are preparing for the best union possible—or in the case of *Braveheart*, the best reunion imaginable. Much like a recipe that requires a sauce to steep for a long time, great relationships often require patience to come about.

Whether you are single, dating, married, divorced or widowed, we all get to wait for the pursuit of the love of the Lord. We go back to the basics of loving God with all our hearts, souls, and minds, and to love one another as ourselves.

Braveheart truly shows that romance is a lifelong story of pursuit.

This pursuit allows the woman to have the soulful respect to follow and encourage her husband wherever he leads!

Wait to pursue or be pursued! It will be the dance of a lifetime and all of heaven's angels will be cheering you on!

THE PASSION IN *THE NOTEBOOK*

Relationships are meant to have passion. Fierce love and passion for one another. In this tale a man sees the woman of his dreams and they instantly connect. After a little Ferris wheel horror and humor, the two lovebirds begin adoring life together. They love each other with everything inside of them.

Though Allie is at first dating another guy, this did not stop Noah the gentleman from risking everything to pursue his love. He climbs up a Ferris wheel and asks her on a date. Then, their friends get involved and set them up on a double date. Talk about good friends.

The love and passion that Allie and Noah had was absolutely contagious. They loved each other being with each other with a fierce passion.

BACHELOR

Congratulations!

We are so thrilled you are able to join us in August. We greatly appreciate your participation, and thank you in advance for your cooperation. We also want to congratulate you for making it to this point!

ABC'S THE BACHELOR

Another jaw-dropping moment in my life and one that offered the opportunity for romance was when a dear friend encouraged me to try out for *The Bachelor*. My friend and boss at the time Kathy urged me to take a leap of faith and try out for this show for a chance to fall in love and to tell people about The Calling.

As soon as I arrived for the audition, I felt extremely intimidated by the thousands of women around me who were also auditioning. I just kept asking God to give me confidence. I filled out the booklet of forms, then it was time for my video audition. That's when divine intervention kicked in: Out of nowhere, God brought the lead casting director over to listen to me answer some of the producers' questions.

Then came the shocker, five months later, after many other steps, forms, background checks and interviews, I was asked to be a finalist on the show. That made me one of the top 35 women out of more than 38,000 who tried out. I knew there were way more qualified ladies that could be there, but God had put me in this group for a reason.

ABC flew me to L.A. for the final interviews. It was the most intense situation of my life. From the moment I walked in I knew I was being scrutinized, with the interviewers looking at my outfit, my style, my tone of voice, everything. The casting director and other decision makers asked to come into my room and see the outfits I planned to wear for the show.

Thing is, I am a fly-by-the-seat-of-my-pants kind of girl. I packed in just an hour the night before leaving, so I didn't have much time to give my choice of outfits much thought, or even think about how the suitcase was organized. My suitcase popped open and out flew several pairs of under garments. I was so embarrassed. Here I was with a casting director and other higher-ups from ABC. Their first impression of me was a pile of clothes on the floor. God keeps me humble, in the most extreme ways. I had to laugh when this happened. That day I learned to always put the delicates on the bottom. Please learn from my mistake, ha!

A few weeks later, I found out I was not chosen for the show, since the producers felt I wouldn't be the best match for the bachelor they'd chosen. Still, the producers and casting director said they would love to keep me in mind for a future episode or another show. I was sad about the final outcome, but also at peace with God's will. I knew He was writing His love story for me, one that would be better than anything in the world.

God took me through the experience of The Bachelor to meet amazing people along the way and see a whole other realm of the world but deep down I knew that I wasn't going to find my true love there. Little did I know about a month later I would meet my true Bachelor, Miles Bradshaw.

TEMPTATIONS THAT COME AND GOD HAS PROTECTED ME

Temptation to Settle - My heart has faced many strong temptations to settle, whether it was meeting charming guys at New Year's Eve parties, church, dancing, mission trips, state functions or coffee shops. There was even an actual chase. One time I was just grabbing a cup of coffee at church and could feel that someone was looking at me. As I started walking out the door, I heard running footsteps right behind me, followed by a suitor eagerly asking me out. I have realized that God just loves making the most of life and does that a lot through other people.

These temptations have been wholeheartedly real most of the time. There have been many guys where I have been able to say no right away, knowing the Holy Spirit has said no. However, there are others where I knew I shouldn't have continued talking to a guy or for that matter go on a date/s with them and have had to learn the hard way. The reason it is so hard is that many pieces of our hearts are given without us even knowing it when being turned down.

Waiting *is hard*. It is one of the hardest things that we have to continually surrender, but I wholeheartedly believe that God truly does have the very best in store for us. I am so grateful I waited for Miles, the one who God had destined for me.

The List. Yes, I know people say to have a list and most commonly they say not to have a list. I believe when having a close relationship with Jesus He tells you the heart desires that He has in store for you for your future spouse. I believe that Jesus is kind enough to show what heart desires He has for each of us! He may show us through meeting another couple or through a certain experience. The experience and heart desire for our future spouse will be coupled with peace, joy and great respect as I have found in Miles.

Many times we don't wait for the desires of our heart, because we think that if someone has 'most' of the characteristics but not all of them, that that is good enough, but I don't think so. We don't think that God is wanting to be that good to us! Really we aren't trusting Him to fulfill the promises that He has placed on our hearts. It all comes back to trusting who God is and that His promises and will for each of our lives are perfect for each of our lives. We need to trust that our God is the perfect storyteller.

I try to write down every heart desire that God confirms to my heart. Many of these heart desires reflect what his character will look like. Even when I witness a situation where I pray that God would instill such a heart into my future spouse.

Now you! What kinds of experiences has God walked you through that left you feeling completely loved and respected? Write it down. This will help you wait for God's best! You can start practicing this in your own life too. Whatever characteristic that you write down, the other person God has for you will most likely want that to be in you too. Don't wait, just love big!

I believe that he or she is out there. And those who are married or widowed write your heart's desires down too, for how you want to love and serve the other person you are married too and or want to be married to.

It is in having my heart desires from God written down, that I was able to not settle. It is not easy though and it is so easy to get entangled in many different things and situations that God doesn't intend for us. Oh and how I have failed many times, but God has been faithful to rescue me every time. He will do the same for you too.

We are meant to wait for God's best. We will know because there will be a light, joyful, heavenly peace that surpasses all understanding when you find your beloved. I felt it and pray you do too. One will know in asking the Holy Spirit if a certain person is their spouse. There will be a whisper to answer. By faith we are meant to listen to that whisper.

Gentlemen, I challenge you to find out which cause you want to pursue to give Jesus ultimate glory in your life. When you know that, and start walking in ultimate faith, you will see your future bride waiting for you to pursue and win her heart. Your future wife wants you to be living out your God-given calling. You may think that it doesn't matter and maybe you both will be able to get along for five, ten, maybe even fifty years, but there will be a yearning deep within your soul if you are not living out those desires deep in your heart. You see they are not there by mistake, they are there to give you great destiny and purpose. You have an unmistakable, unbelievable God-given genetic makeup showing you who you were destined to be.

The ladies are waiting for you, the gentleman, to realize your fullest identity and be all that God has created you to be. We don't want you to be perfect, but we do need you to know who you are in Christ and how to pursue Jesus day in and day out. You see as we know that we know that you will in turn pursue us with an adventurous daring spirit as well as our future family.

Women await the pursuit. The right guy really climbs all the way up to the top of the apple tree to pick you as you wait. While waiting for the man to pursue, get ready. Get ready for the man God has created for you since the beginning of time. Be the beautiful, holy temple God has created you to radiate to the world. Believe that God will combine all those heavenly heart desires into the man you are destined to be with forever. In the meantime, become all you were destined to be.

HOW TO ATTRACT THE RIGHT PERSON

Andy Stanley is a preacher, founder of the North Point Community Church in Alpharetta, Georgia and the author of more than 20 books. For decades he has preached and written about love, success and many other goals that dominate the thoughts of many of us. Amid all of that work, Standley is arguably best known for his one signature catchphrase, one that resonates with me every day: "Become the person that the person you're looking for is looking for!"

I love this concept. It rang especially true during my time preparing and auditioning to become Miss Colorado. The emphasis wasn't so much on having to win, but becoming the best version of myself. It was preached to me that I wasn't competing against anyone, but aiming at becoming all that God has called me to be. Practicing, treating and living out having your body become a Holy Temple.

Couples: We want to see your love story unfold before our very eyes. Live life each day as if it were your last. You will never have a regret. 'Love never fails' (1 Corinthians 13:8). God is love. The love you display to one another with forever be told in eternity!

IN THE WAITING

Wait with gladness and anticipation. I know that along the way, I have been writing postcards to give to my future husband from all the places that Jesus has brought me. I now know that this is Miles and I cannot wait to give them to him that priceless gift on our wedding day. I talk about the things that Jesus has spoken to my heart there and a prayer for a future life together. I have found myself feeling lonely some days and truly wish I was united to my future husband. During these times serving those around has helped and I know will help my future too.

My Nana often encouraged my heart. I remember one time she said to me, "Sweetie, I didn't get married till I was 35 and I feel like I have been married my whole life. There is no hurry." Most of the time it is soul-refreshing to be reminded what the end of the picture looks like, whether that is being married or single. We were made to make the most out of every situation and live out our callings. Before we know it God does bring the desires of our heart to fruition in some form. I believe that there is one true love for each of us, if that is a desire of our heart. We just need to wait upon God's perfect peace to walk into our true soulmate.

CHAPTER 9

The Magic of Making The Most Of Every Situation

> "Whatever life may send your way - make the best of it. Don't waste your time and energy worrying about it. Instead, find a way to do something about it. Learn from it, adjust to it, be strong, be flexible and be your best in every situation."
>
> **- Les Brown**

Every day God gives us the opportunity to make the most out of every moment to leave a life-long legacy. Every difficulty serves to build up our confidence and create an unshakeable conviction that God will be with us in any trouble. He will give us the opportunity to become more like Him in the process. We are able to make the most of everyday by asking

Jesus what He wants us to do in every moment. It may be hard at first to tell but over time it becomes an instinct. What we imagine Jesus doing we then should participate in also. This might be washing the dishes, helping someone across the street, daring to start the business He has echoed on your heart or daring to go away in prayer with Jesus.

Tomorrow is never guaranteed. So why wouldn't I make the most of every day? Why wouldn't I take the chance to say 'hi' to a stranger or buy the person behind me a cup of coffee, go visit my family or go for another degree that I love? If God really is who He says He is I can't help but trust Him every day. Whatever He is putting on my heart to do for His glory I need to pursue. Once I established this fearless mentality it changed my life. I know it will change yours. As Tim McGraw sings, "I went skydiving, I went Rocky Mountain Climbing, I went 2.7 seconds on a bull named Fumanchu, And I loved deeper, And I spoke forgiveness I'd been denying, and he said someday I hope you get the chance to live like you were dying!' Let's live everyday as if we were dying and we will have no regrets.

I started to realize that if I really believe in who my God is, then nothing would be impossible especially in everyday situations. There was no reason not to shoot for the moon and be afraid to miss because God in His genius would string all the missing pieces together perfectly.

K-LOVE MUSIC AWARDS

One time the Lord called me to go to the K-LOVE Fan Awards.

While pursuing God's dream, I found myself in the most beloved of circumstances in the midst of what seemed like a horrible delay.

The awards were in Nashville, Tennessee. I flew out to be there for this exciting event and was then going to travel on another mission to Haiti. I had a hotel room booked for only one evening. After the awards I went to the airport and was shocked to discover that all the flights were overbooked.

I couldn't believe it. I was supposed to be on my way to Haiti at the time. It was so tricky coordinating details to fly down to Haiti in the first place, to the point where arriving on a different day could present serious logistical and even safety concerns. The airport in Port Au Prince, Haiti had been known for kidnappings (especially for Americans). I was also traveling there alone, so this was nerve-wracking. I knew that I needed to trust that God wanted me to be in Tennessee for another day and would orchestrate the new details for my new arrival to Haiti.

I thought of people that I knew in Nashville and asked myself: *What would I do if I knew I could not fail?* As I asked myself this question and the person that came to mind was the one and only Tracie Hamilton. Tracie and her husband, Scott are giants in the faith. Scott was an Olympic Gold Medalist in figure skating, but had to fight through four recurrences of cancer. Tracie had overcome her share of challenges too. I met the Hamilton family through a dear friend, former NFL wide receiver David Nelson, who has a nonprofit in Haiti, I'mMe to help Haiti.

I contacted Tracie and asked if there was any way I could stay with them for the evening. She wrote back and said of course I could. Before I knew it, I had arrived at the Hamilton's' lovely home. Their nanny walked me to my guest room and told me who had just recently stayed there: The President of Haiti and his wife!

I could hardly believe it. Only God could coordinate such amazing details. I also found out that the Hamilton's had two adopted children from Haiti. God was using what seemed like a horrible delay and turned it into a major life confirmation.

God is our master networker! When He gives you a dream He will also give you a plan for how to execute it.

WALKING THROUGH JESUS' EYE

I believe that we are in a true season where Jesus is ushering Himself into this world. He is coming in as the risen King. There was a time where Jesus made Himself known to me that He wanted me to walk through His eyes. I was going through a season of life where I was being followed by crows. This may seem like a normal thing. But I could feel the demonic oppression that these crows were carrying (Ephesians 6:10-11).

One morning I heard the most disturbing sound, that of a crying hurting baby mixed in with a bird squawk. I looked up from my bed and there was literally the biggest crow I had ever seen staring straight at me crowing with this horrific sound. It was as if Satan himself was in this crow. This was much like the scene where in the movie, The Passion, the baby looks over at Jesus while being crucified and smiles.

I declared three times that the evil spirit be gone in Jesus' name, and it finally left. All to say, this was a very hard spiritual warfare type of season.

That very next day I had three different people share with me that they heard the Lord say that I needed to step away from everything and just be with Jesus. Jesus had something really special to share with me. I had peace about this and postponed all appointments. I sat with The Lord in my bedroom and just began to worship Him.

Throughout the last couple of years prior to this Jesus had been revealing Himself to me by showing me His eye and sometimes His beautiful face. I had started seeing Jesus' beloved face in this time of worship and as my heart came into a full heart surrender and a surrender of complete peace to His will for me. I would most often see His right eye. As I gazed into His beautiful eye and face, I too saw Jesus look like that of the famous child prodigy known from heaven.

In looking at the details and beauty of Jesus' eyes I saw that it changed sometimes - but it was that of blue and green and as I really looked and saw I saw that it was Earth in His eye. Then, in the middle of it one can see the galaxies of the universe. I had continued to see Jesus' eyes as my heart worshipped Him in a wholehearted surrender.

I saw that Jesus was sharing something very special with me. He wanted me to walk through His eye. I said, Jesus, how in the world do you want me to do this? He said, Chrysandra, by faith you can walk through my eye. After seeing that this really was what He wanted me to do, it was as if my soul physically stepped into heaven. I literally walked through His right eye.

I walked through and saw first a whole bunch of extremely tall walls and floor of clouds. I was walking on clouds and by these tall cotton like steam clouds. I was in awe of this scene. Then in a moment it changed to a garden. It changed to that of a garden where there were a whole bunch of roses but these roses were that of pink and purple where there were no more thrones. Jesus reminded me there that there were no thrones in heaven. He took them all away especially given the crown of thorns on Earth by those that He was saving for eternity.

I could even smell the sweet aroma of the roses in the garden. It smelt like very fresh flowers under the sun in one flower with an extra dose of rose. It was gorgeous. All I could see were the hills of these beloved roses.

Then all of a sudden I found myself on top of a pillar and saw that there were seven more of them in front of me. I saw that on the eighth pillar there was a massive figure and I could tell it was an angel. I could tell it was a male angel and he was gesturing to come towards Him. I hopped from one staggered pillar to the next. I was asking Jesus to make sure I wouldn't be afraid when I met this angel. Then it was finally time to jump to the last pillar, where the angel was waiting, arms open wide.

I leapt and was hugged by this massive creature. I couldn't believe it. I could see the squareness of his jaw line, but there was a blurring glory over his face.

He said, "Hi Chrysandra, my name is Michael." At this time, I had no idea about angels in the Bible. All I knew is that God had angels come to people often and I heard something about Gabriel the angel, but nothing else. All to say when He said this I just thought he was an angel of Jesus Christ.

He started to speak: "Chrysandra, you need to know that all of heaven's armies are behind you. We are here to help you. We were here, you just have to send us. We are on your side. You need to know that you must go forward with The Calling. This is a dream from God's heart to yours and you are meant to live it out. Even if the battle looks unbearable, know that we are here with you fighting on your behalf. You physically could have very little people, but you really in real heavenly reality have the best army. Nothing is too hard for our God!"

I couldn't believe what I was hearing, but I needed to hear it, with all the years of warfare that had been going on. I then saw Jesus' eye again and He told me to open my eyes. I opened my eyes and was in awe. I wrote everything down and trusted by faith that this would happen. I also knew that I had never heard of anyone around me at the time going to heaven and coming back and that this was a sacred adventure.

The next morning I woke up and immediately went through my Beth Moore bible study materials on Daniel. That very day I was going into Chapter 10. Beth Moore was giving an intro to this Chapter and I couldn't believe what I was hearing. She started talking about Michael the

Archangel. The Angel of all the heavenly Armies. I was astounded. God was validating everything that I just had heard in heaven through his word. I had no knowledge of Michael before this and God was showing me that this was truly from Him. He took me to heaven to breath His fresh breath of encouragement!

Here's more Michael commentary: "*The archangel*—This word occurs but once more in the sacred writings, namely, 1 Thessalonians 4:16. So that, whether there be one archangel only, or more, it is not possible for us to determine. Michael is called *one of the chief princes,* Daniel 10:13, and *the great prince,* Daniel 12:1; (on which passages see the notes.) And, because it is said, (Revelation 12:7,) that Michael and his angels fought against the dragon and his angels, Estius conjectures that Michael is the chief or prince of all the angels. But this argument is not conclusive."

This was the beginning of Jesus showing me that in this heart posture of true surrender that I and His children will find ultimate revelation and wisdom. God has ever since then been taking me to heaven when He chooses and reveals the great unknown.

I share all this to say that I believe in the return of our great King Jesus, as that is new on my calendar we see that Jesus has ultimate revival and dream casting in store.

"God's children will dream His dreams and see His visions." - Acts 16

In the Return of our King it will become extremely dark, but the light will shine even brighter. I believe that in trusting Jesus with all that He tells us in these intimate moments, we see that we are born to live out these dreams, by faith and this will usher in the Red Sea miracles that we are meant to bring in as Jesus' bride to humanity.

We must choose which side we are going to be on and then, walk by faith like never before every single day! God is rising up His armies in Heaven, but also on Earth. You are invited to play a mighty role in God's story. You are meant to be a main character that means making the most of every day and every moment.

Are you ready? Are you ready to trust Jesus with every fiber of your being to live out your calling?

CHAPTER 10
Activation Sheet

Activation Sheet

> 'Behold, I am coming soon. My reward is with me,
> and I will give to everyone according to what he
> has done. I am the Alpha and the Omega, the First
> and the Last, the Beginning and the End!'
>
> **- Revelation 22**

It is finally time to let ourselves adventure into releasing and activating our true God-given calling's. The way to activate our calling is to have the end in mind. One day we will be face to face with Jesus. Can you imagine the glory of that time and the joy to be with the One our souls were made for? What do we want Him to say to you? This could be 100 years from now, it could be next year or even later today and we will be before our Savior. However long, we will be face to face with Jesus. The question is, will we hear 'well done!' Will we live out what He puts in our hearts to do with Him on this earth to display His splendor.

As in any grand anecdotes and life stories let's start a new milestone in yours. Let's think of our most famous heroes and the gifts they were given. Each of these characters needed to awaken their gifts and talents to begin living out their calling. Imagine Superman not using his strength or Spiderman not using his web. Each hero needs to decide to use their soul power to help the world around them. Hulk decided using his might to help the world, Thor decided to use the hammer given to him, and Wonder Woman used the lasso to defend the helpless. God has given you many 'powers' to help the world. Now is the time to activate your calling to help impact God's kingdom around the globe. You are believed in.

The main ingredient of activation is that of belief. Belief in knowing that God has called us to something bigger than ourselves. Even when the prophet Samuel came to find the upcoming king of Israel He found the most unlikely, David, who was still a shepherd. David was meant to be King. God was calling him into the journey of his destiny to prepare him for who he was destined to become.

When we know that God has breathed a dream from His heart to ours and knowing He believes in us to fulfill it, there is nothing that can stop it from happening. And it's the same with people in their everyday lives. God made everything on purpose, especially you. Every circumstance is meant for us to mold our character in Jesus'.

You are here at a particular moment in time to do something that only you can do to impact the world in a way that it's best done by you. You have your purpose and calling to live out. Now all you have to do is 'identify your calling.' This calling is the journey that God has decided for us to fulfill our unique superpowers and our capabilities to display His glory. Everything that we live through in our daily lives is part of our journey in this world. It is also part of our spiritual journey, which God is building for us. As it progresses, we find our calling along the way. The goal is to never give up on what God has said He wants to fulfill.

LESSONS FROM GIDEON

As mentioned at the beginning of this book, the story of Gideon is one of overcoming astronomical odds to prevail. Taking a 300-man army to battle against an army 100 times larger requires an enormous amount of courage, regardless of what the final outcome might be. Gideon's ability to muster the courage to take his tiny army to victory shows how God can help us accomplish goals that might otherwise seem impossible.

What is your 300? What sort of miracle do you need from Jesus? This message of Gideon, The Calling, and I all to point to Jesus ... the author and creator of our heavenly destiny!

Gideon was a foreshadowing of Jesus himself. Gideon was one of the weakest, most unlikely of heroes. He had no chance without God by his side. We too get to be foreshadows and ambassadors of Jesus Christ.

We overcome adversity by the blood of the lamb and the word of our testimony, so start proclaiming your destiny! Proclaim what God has done for Gideon, proclaim what Jesus has done for You and what He has promised you in His word.

HOW TO FOLLOW YOUR DREAMS

> "The only place where your dream becomes impossible is in your own thinking." **– Robert Schuller**

Dreaming is a necessity in our walk with Jesus Christ. Listening and dreaming with our heavenly Father of what He wants, for it allows us to see the world through His eyes. When we view life through our heavenly Father's eyes, it reveals the opportunities, truth and our true identity found only in Him. In Him, we are inspired, empowered and equipped to do all that we are called to do.

The importance of our imagination is vital. God gave us our imagination for a very important reason for it is a part of Jesus' heart. Just like he gave us eyes to see, hands to touch, a nose to smell, he gave us our imagination to create. We use all our other senses several times a day if we are able, but how often do we use our imaginations?

When we live life with Godly vision we bring glory to Him out of a pureness of heart that is fueled by faith. Just like the aspen tree leaves applaud when the wind blows or when a child laughs at a funny face, all of these interactions are characteristics of our Father. We as human beings are meant to live an extraordinary life. If we aren't willing to imagine and dream it is possible you will miss special details of your calling. So color outside the lines.

We were branded with our heavenly Father's authority. We have to know that there is nothing that is impossible with Him. Thus, we have the freedom to dream. Now this may mean that we could fail, but we shouldn't be afraid to try; we should be afraid *not* to try. For what we do here on Earth will echo throughout all eternity. We are taking care of our soul when we dream with our heavenly Father. It awakens our senses to His perspective on Earth.

TURNING DREAMS INTO ACTION

Now let's take those ideas and apply some practical tools to the task of dreaming.

Go out take your dreaming supplies. This may mean taking your colored pencils, earphones to listen to your favorite genre of music, traveling to a scene of inspiration (some folks are inspired by the atmosphere of wood chips on the floor, others are inspired by looking down a ocean pier. Whatever it may be, make sure to stretch your imagination regularly. It should be a regular routine to be irregular. One gets better with dreaming as one practice.

One time the Lord had me sit with Him. He whispered to my heart. "Chrysandra, do you know that you can start creating in heaven, just like you can create on Earth?" The Holy Spirit awakened my heart to understand what He was saying to me. He was saying that we can create in heaven, for that is our ultimate reality and us as children of God are able to do so.

That is our ultimate job position. It is almost like Earth is our internship and heaven is our official career launch. Can you imagine what we can do here on Earth while knowing we can create in heaven. Maybe God will impress on your heart to build the largest jungle gym treehouse in heaven that one has ever seen, including animals in different sections, tea party rooms, knight training rooms, a universe lookout room. Or maybe you are meant to come up with one of heaven's play productions. Can you imagine the cast you can choose from? How exciting is that? Heaven is our ultimate reality.

Remember when you were little? You dreamt of being a princess or a superhero? When you had these dreams, you acted them out. There was no hiding of what you really wanted to become or do. You dared to live it. You pulled from the supplies about you and you believed it.

Depending on how long you held onto these dreams you most likely had those that loved you come around and speak life into your dreams. Perhaps they bought you animations that brought that dream to life in a way you ever thought possible. Maybe they bought you an outfit to meet that dream.

You see, our dreams attract activation. If we really believe in something, we are able to start living it out. This is why dreaming is so important. We are able to see that our imaginations truly do create our future realities. What we dream about most likely becomes our very reality.

This is why it is so important for us to dream big. I mean to dream bigger than ever before. Our reality with God is that all things are possible, with Him and through Him.

These can't be selfish dreams. They are meant to be dreams matching the top two commandments - to love God and love each other. If your dream matches this, then my friend this is a God dream. It is a dream from His heart to yours.

Jesus wanted us to look at Him and see that all things were possible with Him and for Him. If we really believe in Him and love Him, we want to be able to bring Him the most glory.

The question really is what do we want to be doing with Him forever and ever? How do we want to spend eternity? It is when we are able to imagine spending eternity with Jesus and what we will be doing in our real home that we can begin to really dream and live out those dreams here on Earth.

We need to know that dreams come from imagining what could be? What is something that God wants to do?

As in anything, our dreaming muscle must be exercised. We must practice dreaming beginning with listening – it's then that we find our ultimate purpose.

Listen to your heart, always. Imagine the greatness of infinite possibilities. Ask yourself: "What would you do if you knew you could not fail?"

OPENING THE TOOLBOX

This book comes with all sorts of tools that you can use to help you follow your dreams and pursue your calling. We will start with an item that comes with every copy of The Calling: a dream card!

Please pull out your dream card. I invite the Holy Spirit to speak straight from His heart to yours, to enlighten us to His plan and to make sure we stick to His plan.

I am going to give you a couple minutes to fill out your dream cards. Don't leave without writing down your dream, or dreams.

Next, consult a world map on your computer or phone. This map shows the potential of souls He wants you to touch in this world. If you are able to print the world map. You can pinpoint where God has taken you in the world, and where you want to go. Use this map as an aspirational tool, for all the adventures you want to take in the future.

ACTIVATION QUESTIONS

Read through these questions carefully. Think about what they mean to you, then take the time to answer each of them with as much consideration and mindfulness as you can.

What would you do if you knew you could not fail?

What do you feel like God is calling you to do?

What cause would you be willing to give up your life for, knowing that God has put this burning passion on your heart for a reason?

What would be a way that you could tie in all these passions into a vision of bringing God the most glory?

What are some vision ideas that God could use to bring Him the most glory possible?

In no more than 15 words, what is your personal vision statement?

What are some tangible, actionable steps that you would need to take to make your dreams come true?

ACTION TIMELINE

I_____(fill in your name here) _____
will aim to achieve my personal goal by _____(fill in your target date here)_____

God's Fingerprints: How has Jesus shown you that this is what He wants you to do (through scripture and experiences)? Who is going to keep you accountable in pursuing this Calling God has put on your heart?

Accountability Partner's Name: _____

For more information on how to activate your dreams and find your calling, visit our website at www.thecallingnonprofit.org

CHAPTER 11
Calling Boot Camp

Becoming a Callingineer!

"The Great I AM gave you an EXTRAordinary God-given dream. It is time for you to live it out!"

Yes. We are finally here. Let's do this. Let's become CALLINGIEERS!

Callingieers meaning those fearlessly living out our God-given calling's!

Whenever we talk about improving something for ourselves, be it our physical fitness or our mental well-being, there is one word that often comes up - boot camp. The word is often used by militaries in their training to make sure a person is fit enough to fight the enemy and the ones in the wrong. Interestingly, if we apply the idea of boot camps of our spirituality as we rejuvenate it, we could be fighting the enemy to our soul.

Building on the theme from the previous chapter, the goal of this boot camp is to pursue your calling fearlessly. Here's a look at what you can do to find your calling! Let us dive into a seven-day boot camp to launch your calling. The hope is for this to become a weekly guide for you to use to live out your calling day in and day out. Here's a brief breakdown.

Day 1 – Believe - Inspire / Rekindle the Seed of the Dream

Day 2 – Generosity - Give freely; those who give will receive

Day 3 – The Power of Obedience- (Power & Anointing to walk in our weaknesses)

Day 4 – Environment Create and thrive in an environment of growth (scenery, people, activities, rest, etc.)

Day 5 - Day to Fast - Today, the goal is to fast and pray for Jesus to open miracles as only He can help you achieve your God-given dream.

Day 6 - Thinking about Mortality – Today I will go to a cemetery. What do you want your tombstone to say?

Day 7 - Day to Rest and Celebrate

Calling Tools: Music, Journal, God's Word, Location, Earbuds, favorite inspirational books, people.

REFLECTIONS ON BOOTCAMP:

To frame these exercises, let's return to the central question of the book, and of The Calling: What would you do if you knew you could not fail? Now ask yourself this: What would you do if you knew without a shadow of a doubt that you were born to do something that no one has ever done?

The question is, do we really believe? Do we believe that God is who He says he is?

Remember when you were four years old and nothing seemed

impossible, because your imagination and faith filled in the gaps? This is what I believe Jesus means by living out our child-like faith.

We are born to create and imagine. If something isn't in front of us right now, our faith can help manifest it at the proper time—the same way mom and dad might have brought your 4-year-old self an ice cream when you started imagining one in your hands. The thing is, parents don't know how much their children want something, until they voice their desires and even their imaginations. The same goes for God and His children. Having a relationship with the great I AM of the Universe through His son Jesus Christ, we find that our imaginations are a gift from Him to us. Yes, the dreams in our heart are from God. Are you ready to start imagining today?

Now, just as you would work out physically to improve your strength, agility, and health, you can shape and develop your imagination.

> "The Disney Imagineers, renowned for their ability to turn fantastical ideas into magical realities, confront creative challenges every day. They do so—and succeed – utilizing time-proven techniques and a belief that anything can be achieved if the mind is freed from conventional formulas!" - The Imagineering Workout, by the Disney Imagineers

> "… Adapting the mental processes and creative techniques the Imagineers have honed over many years to your own home your own life!"

- The Imagineering Workbook by Disney's Imagineers

Imagining is part of God's very heart on this Earth. We are meant to think of creative solutions for solving problems. Whether a challenge involves your family, your job or even a traffic jam, your imagination and ingenuity are there to guide you. Our minds and souls are born to create and to solve problems. The incredible thing about this process of dreaming is that we each have a unique individual lens that allows us to see life in a different way. All of our backgrounds have different mixtures of people, environments, cultures, tragedies, successes and all have shaped what we value and believe in.

What if our imaginations are what are the propellers in causing the

God given future destined to be lived out and God is letting you play a HIStoric role? Don't let Him cast someone else, He wants to pick YOU!

Can you imagine what the world would look like if each of us were to pursue our own personal dream, the one that lies deep in our hearts. The one that God put us on this Earth to find?

We know that God has given us breath in our lungs and a purpose to love Him and others with all of our hearts. When we are doing this, we will find our God-given calling lying right in front of us. The average lifespan in America is just shy of 80 years. If we round up to 80 years, that works out to about 25 billion seconds and breaths in our lungs to fill in. What can we do with all of those seconds to live our best lives, and to glorify God?

If these are the criteria for people around the world to be able to create, how much can we create and invent as God's beloved Sons and Daughters? If we truly believe that God is who He says He is, then how can we get away from the individual purpose that He puts on each of our lives to love Him and His people with selfless, wholehearted love?

Much as Walt Disney conceived of a world involving Imagineers, God's brilliant creation calls on us to be his Callingineers. We are called to dream, not just while we sleep, but in our waking hours when we imagine our futures. Once we see that our lives are found in Him, then we are forced to realize that this life that we live is not our own. It is His, God's! This is the pivotal point where our selfish-driven lives begin to be shaped into Holy lives!

The major difference between these two kinds of lives, and the reason why this method has been proven to work for thousands of people, is that you know what you know what you are being called to do. Not your parents, your boss, your spouse or friends—YOU! In that way, the process doesn't necessarily show your gifts, strengths, talents and weaknesses. Instead it reveals what you are truly destined to do! In this boot camp you will find what you were born to do. It will be a pivotal change in your life.

Now this is your warning. Like an Army boot camp, this is not going to be easy. But these exercises, questions and reflection sections will enable you to know what you were born to do and let you take action and the steps of faith to make the changes needed to walk in your calling. No matter what stage of life you're at, you can pursue your God-given calling, the one that only you were born to live out! Now we are getting excited for you!

This won't only change you, it will also change everyone you come across. You will become the true game-changer you are called to be. You are meant to change the game. When it looks like a loss in a situation you get to stand up, when you see someone cheated, you get to give. You will be asking God to give you His lens for humanity, then you will be sparked to change the world all around you with great humility and love for God and others.

So now that you know what's at stake, will you take the leap with us to find your calling!? We promise you will never be the same and you will live a life of no regrets! Get ready to be transformed.

Here's what the process looks like:

> God gives you a dream
>
> God develops one's character to fulfill the dream (this usually requires trials)
>
> You preserve and continue walking in pureness of heart, not giving up
>
> The God-given Dream is fulfilled!
>
> The process begins again.

"Aim at heaven and you will get Earth thrown in. Aim at Earth and you get neither." – Lewis

DAY 1: MADE TO DREAM

Let's Spark Your Dream. The first step into the calling is the dream that you have. God has given us many messages in the Bible that talk about this dream and the importance that it entails. Here are a few that you can read and also fill in the blank with what your heart and mind tell you.

Ideal Location: Bookstore or Library

(go to a quiet place where you feel at peace)
- Jeremiah 29:11 ESV

For I know the _____ I have for you, declares the Lord, plans for _____ and not for evil, to give you a _____ and a hope.
- Proverbs 16:3 ESV

Commit your _____ to the Lord, and your plans will _____.
- Matthew 6:33 ESV

But seek first the kingdom of God and his righteousness, and _____ these things will be _____ to you.
- Psalm 37:4 ESV

Delight yourself in the Lord, and he will give you the _____ of your heart.
Today we are going to go to your favorite bookstore or library. Time allocated when you walk through the door: 30-45 minutes. In the meanwhile, read through and check the lists wherever deemed necessary and encircle whenever needed. When you're done, put a big checkmark here:

[   ]

While you look through the books on the shelves, ask yourself the big question:

STEP 1

Discover a book in the store, library or your telephone in the event that you should that has a guide of the world.

Did you discover it? Yes / No

While you look through the books on the shelves, ask yourself the big question:

STEP 1:

Find a book in the store, library, or your phone if you must that has a map of the world.

Did you find it? Yes / No

Ok now look closely at the map and look at different parts of the world, imagine yourself being there. Imagine yourself being in several different spots. Think about what you see, taste, smell, and feel.

Which location did you love being at the most?
_____

Pretend that you are there right now in that location with Jesus. For the remainder of our time today I want you to pretend you were in that location. What is Jesus speaking over you? What is He confirming? What is He wanting to change? What dream is He showing you?
_____

Now that you're done with that exercise, consider this: Have you ever truly absorbed the fact that absolutely no one ever has been created like you? You are one of a kind. You are not just one in 7.8 billion. Think about that for a minute.

Ok, now that your uniqueness has sunk in, take a moment to assess your current mood.

Circle all that comes to mind:

Inspired
Bewildered
Speechless
Astounding
Overwhelming

By recognizing how special and valued you are no matter how you might 'feel' in the moment, you start to see that you have a unique glorious purpose, a God-given destiny to fulfill.

Today you get to imagine what could be. It is time to go around the library or bookstore and pick up books that inspire you! This can be any kind of book, general, historic, magazines, even books aimed at kids or teens. Walk around for about 10 minutes and make yourself a comfy seat on the ground, by a window, coffee table and write down the top seven books that inspire you the most:

1.
2.
3.
4.
5.
6.
7.

What types of themes do you see in these books? Which characters do you like the most? Whose legacy would you want to fulfill if you could choose any in those books?

_____

Now just pick your top two. What do you respect and admire about those two books the most? Which character from a book would you want to be your mentor?

Character's Name:
Book's Name:

_____

Now the question lies in asking, what kind of legacy do you want to leave on this Earth?

What kinds of trouble do you see on this Earth?

How would you address these problems?

Who would you ask to take on the journey?

If your life were a book, what would you want people to read about you?

The truth of the matter is that we are each given by God a backdrop and platform to live out our individual purpose.

At the end of Day 1, we will leave you with these questions:

What would you do if you knew you could not fail to love God and humanity?

Where would you be?

Who would be with you?

What would you be doing?

Has this idea come to mind in the past?

What has stopped you from following through?

Task for the rest of the day: Imagine yourself living out this answer from your heart to God!

Finally, post the following on social media:

Take a picture of yourself and say you were in _____ (the location you imagine). Now declare a cause you want to fight for. This should be simple, short, and inspirational.

#Callingineer #imaginetheimpossible

See you tomorrow!

DAY 2: MADE TO CREATE

Directions: Go to your favorite hotel lobby!

Today we are going to go to your favorite hotel lobby. Time allocated when you walk through the door: 30-45 minutes. When you're done, put a big check mark here:

[   ]

Go to the lobby and order a drink (coffee, water, tea, pop, whatever you like). I am not sure about you but there is just nothing like being in a hotel lobby. It makes our brains and souls somehow believe we are on vacation even if we are only 5 to 10 minutes away from our home.

Once you are settled let's begin.

I, _____, am here for such a time as this (Esther 4:14)

QUESTIONS: What would you do if you knew you could not fail?

Our first question to begin this adventure is asking what would you do if you knew you could not fail!? What would you be willing to give up your life for?

Ask yourself this question nine times:

WHAT would I do if I knew I could not fail!?
What WOULD I do if you knew I could not fail!?
What would I do if I knew I could not fail!?
What would I DO is I knew I could not fail?
What would I do IF I knew I could not fail?
What would I do if I knew I could not fail?
What would I do if I knew I COULD not fail?
What would I do if I knew I could NOT fail?
What would I do if I knew I could not FAIL!?

Now that you've asked this question, what first comes to mind?

What do you see?

Can you describe what you see with more detailed words?

Time for some more questions:

Who are the people in your inner circle?

Who are the people in your life that you look up to and want to emulate?

Who are the people in your life that give you energy?

Who are the people in your life who drain your energy?

Who are the people in your life that God put there?

Today, text that small number of people you want to emulate and ask to bring them a treat. Kindness opens the doors to king hearts. If you want to be like that person, it is time to serve them. Watch the doors open to you in due time, when you offer kindness and generosity.

"As a prisoner for the lord, then, I urge you to live a life worthy of the calling you have received!" (Ephesians 4:1)

What do you feel like God is calling you to do? What cause would you be willing to give up your life for, knowing that God has put this burning passion on your heart for a reason?

What would be a way that you could tie in all these passions into a vision of bringing God the most glory?

What are some vision ideas that God could use to bring Him the most glory possible? What is your vision statement (write it in 10 to 15 words)?

What are some action steps that you would need to take to make this happen? Who would you need to contact?

God's Fingerprints: How has Jesus shown you that this is what He wants you to do (through Scripture and Experiences)?

Who is going to keep you accountable in pursuing this Calling God has put on your heart?

Name of Calling ACTIVATOR (you): _____

Accountability Partner: _____

Date: _____

DAY 3: SEEK OUT NATURE

Good morning, God's Dreamer. Today is your adventure day. Go to where you are closest to the sunrise.

Directions: Go to your favorite creative spot. This could be a park or a zoo, preferably.

If now you could go to a park, backyard, or the top of a mountain.

However, if you can, it is highly encouraged to go to the nearest zoo[21].

Once you are inside find a sit by one of your favorite animals and open up this page again.

Think about the difference in all animals. Watch the zebras, giraffes, polar bears, penguins, and seals. Listen to their sounds, take in their smells. Drink in every drop of God's creativity, from heads to tails. This isn't the longest of days in the boot camp, but certainly an important one. It is one that will make you understand nature a little better. When you can

---

[21] *I seek out hard things. I tried to imitate other singers. It was a self-discovery for me to move from imitating others to me growing to sing in my own voice. The opera was difficult and it felt like a personal conquest.* **Daniela Vega**

be grateful for God's creation throughout the world especially in living creatures we get a glimpse of inspiration for the magnitude of imagination our God really has.

What creature caught your attention the most?
_____

What does the Internet have to say about that creature? What is its purpose?
_____

If you could imagine with God what you want your life to look like, what would that be?

How can you stretch your dream in this season to match God's creative nature?

When you're done, put a big check mark here and move to the next day:

[   ]

DAY 4: DAY TO FAST

Day to Fast

Today the goal is to fast and pray for Jesus to open miracles like only He can for your God given dream.

What do you feel like you can give up today? Social media? Food? A special food or drink for the day?

When you're done, put a big check mark here:

[   ]

Today, notice the environment, the climate. What is it like?
_____
_____

What is the dream God is putting on your heart?
_____
_____

DAY 5: DAY TO SERVE

There is no calling without the art and blessing of serving. This is serving God and others above ourselves.

"Your greatness is not what you have; it's what you give."- Mother Teresa

Most of the time, God opens doors while we are serving others. Sometimes this seems similar to our dreams. Other times, it seems completely contrary to achieving our dreams, but you see dreams come alive when we help others. Maybe you could help watch a family's kiddos, maybe help a friend move, maybe take someone who is lonely today on a walk and a cup of coffee! How can you love someone today and serve them? The questions could go on for a while, and you need to understand that the answers to these questions are the answers that God has sent our way for us to be closer to our calling.

- Who needs your help today?
- Who can you go out of your way to serve? Does someone come to mind? Now go!
- I would challenge you to give a whole day (or at least many hours) to help that person.
- Who did you serve today and why?
  _____
  _____

- What did you do? What did you learn?
  _____
  _____

DAY 6: DAY TO REFLECT

Today, go to a cemetery. Sit quietly and reflect on this question: What do you want your tombstone to say?

Father? Mother? Friend? History maker? Now write out what you would want people to read about you at your funeral. Would you want them to say how kind you are? Would you want them to talk about how you served the world?

How do you want to be remembered? Are you living your life right now in such a way that will help you achieve those goals?

DAY 7: DAY TO REST

On your day to rest and celebrate, grab your journal and something to write with. Go somewhere quiet, where you can hear Jesus in the best and clearest way possible. Write down what God says to you, and what faith means to you. Rest, reflect, even meditate if that helps you get in touch with your spirituality, and sense of self.

Once you've done that quiet period of rest and reflection, go and celebrate all the ways that God has been faithful in your life. Celebrate the promises He has placed on your heart and thank Him in advance for all of them coming into being. He who can called you in faithful. Now is your time to walk into all that He has called you to be.

Ask yourself, 'What is God calling me to do?'

Then ask, 'How can I go after my calling today?'

Become the Callingieer that Jesus has destined you to be not tomorrow, or next week. Right now is your time!

CONCLUSION

You were meant to read this book for such a time as this. God has a unique calling just for you to live out that no one is meant to do in all time and history but you! Forever know that nothing is impossible with our great God and that voice inside of you sharing not to be afraid is Jesus. He loves you and has an incredible calling for you to live out even throughout Heaven. Know you have 'The Calling' family, me and all other 'Callingieers' cheering you on. Let's live out our God-given calling's together! #wwydiykycnf

Other Resources & Tools from The Calling:
The Activation *Dream Kit*
Training Videos on Living Your Calling from Chrysandra
Activation Sheet
All Calling Products

All these Resources & much more will be found on The Calling's website: www.thecallingnonproft.org

THE CALLING'S HISTORY

2007 – April 11th Conference at The Rock of Southwest Baptist Church in Littleton, Colorado: included Danny Oertli, Chrysandra Brunson, Focus on the Family, K-Love Radio with Jen Lohman, Way FM, McDonald's, Bear Creek High School, Foothills Bible Church, Christian rapper LaJay, The Rock of Southwest, and many others.

National Media: Focus on the Family, Brio Magazine article written about the first Calling event of 2007

2009 – April 10th Conference at Civic Center Park, Denver Colorado: Speakers: Bryan Schwartz (former NFL player), Brian Brown (founder of Park Church Denver), Josh Weidman (author, pastor and speaker), Everfound (K-Love Artist), Desperation Band, Christian rapper Keithon Stribling, Christian band Rough Draft, Make a Wish Foundation, Starbucks, Colorado Christian University, Denver Rescue Mission, CCU Roomies, Friends and Volunteers and many others.

Civic Center Park, Denver, Colorado April 10, 2009

2010 – The Calling became a ministry at Colorado Christian University, led by Chrysandra Brunson and made up of incredible students from the university, professor advisors including Dr. Greg Green and others at the university. Endorsed by former US Senator Bill Armstrong and community members including Jim Weidman, Jim Copeland and Sharon Kitzmiller. Hosted workshops and retreats with Camp Idrahaje, Colorado Christian University, refugees from around the nations alongside Ignite Ministries, Foothills Bible Church and more. Partnered with many organizations and resources like The CALL Vocational and Life Purpose Guide from Follow Your Calling LLC. The Calling continued as a ministry at Colorado

Christian University and was filed as its own nonprofit 501(c)3 entity with the state of Colorado in August of 2010.

Students participated in The Calling's ministry at CCU starting in 2010 and Hosted The Calling's event at Civic Center Park in Denver Colorado

The Calling's event at Red Rocks Amphitheater in Morrison, Colorado with Switchfoot and Chasen April 16, 2011. The Calling's event at Red Rocks Amphitheater in Morrison, Colorado April 16, 2011. Shortly after this epic event, The Calling sustained a series of unfortunate events that caused a temporary slowdown for the ministry. A large portion of the funds raised were discovered stolen by someone who was close to the nonprofit, and then Chrysandra was diagnosed with Lyme disease. Despite what felt like desperate circumstances, the vision carried on throughout that broken season and continued to have a strong presence in Colorado and across America.

SUMMARY Dream of 2007 – 2015

Reaching and touching over 7 million hearts since its inception, The Calling has continued to host events and have a presence coast to coast in the U.S. from California to New York and in between (including Missouri, California, Texas, Washington DC and so many other special places) and in Haiti and Israel,. Partnering with many global companies to get the news out including SONY, TBN, K-LOVE Radio, Google, Disney, MACY'S, MLB, The United States Congress, and others still in progress! They have been invited to speak at schools, churches, prayer breakfasts, media and global nonprofit and business events and more. All of these partnerships and outlets are focused on helping humanity live out God's unique dreams for individual lives.

2012 – Chrysandra won the title of People's Choice Miss Colorado and used the platform to feature The Calling and its mission and vision. Through Miss Colorado, The Calling and Chrysandra were invited as the keynote speaker for events like Sonlight Christian Camp for 4th and 5th graders in the Rocky Mountains. The Calling continued to be a presence and provide resources at events like Bandimere speedway, the

Western Conservative Summit and more. This year also marked the first trip to Haiti to start planning the Global Conference in Port Au Prince with Cherry Hills Church. This started the process of developing strong partnerships with the organizations and people of Haiti as well as visits to the Haitian Embassy in Washington DC.

Chrysandra speaking at Sonlight Christian Camp in Pagosa Springs, Colorado 2012

2013 – The Calling's message was shared on a public platform with over 40,000 Haitians, major political leaders, Billy Graham Crusade coordinators and the like at an organized event in Haiti. Organizations and individuals came together to really see the dream for The Calling for the people of Haiti. The Christian Movement for a New Haiti became a strong organization to partner with as well as many others. Two million Haitians were touched through a broadcast on El Shalom Haitian Radio. In Colorado, The Calling continued to have a presence and impact on the local community as well with the annual 4th of July event at Bandimere Speedway also presence at the Western Conservative Summit.

2014 – The Calling was invited by The Navigators as a guest speaker on a platform to reach over 100,000 people across the United States. This year brought more travel to Haiti for additional conference planning. The Calling was also invited to bring guest speakers at Jim Elliot Christian School and provide a keynote speaker for a weekend retreat for Vail Christian School as well as holding several community events to encourage others to live out their callings. *Morrison Town Event, Morrison, Colorado 2014*

Highlight: Our beloved Bev. We helped her find her calling of teaching women to make sleeping bags/coats for the homeless. This is the business plan that she created at age 70!

2015 – The Calling was invited to provide a keynote speaker at the Jefferson County Prayer Breakfast with more than 300 in attendance including U.S. senators. They also sent a keynote speaker in St. Louis, Missouri for those in their 70s to 100s and mission groups in the area as well as a keynote speaker to Marilyn Hickey's young adults and then seized an opportunity to speak to over 5 million Haitians via radio. The Calling staff was able to travel to gather partners for the upcoming Global Conference in Haiti including Scott and Traci Hamilton, Mac Powell from Third Day, i'mMe located in the US and Haiti (I'mMe founded by and including NFL players). They were able to travel back to Haiti with representatives to help The Calling's Global Conference including representatives from Google, The Boston Red Sox, National Magazine and Video Media. They were able to share the vision and the message with those in Haiti with over 5 million on Radio & TV networks. They provided seminars on entrepreneurship, marketing and finding your God given calling. The Calling also hosted a free evening called a Night of Inspiration with former Boston Red Sox motivational speaker Rex Crain. They also continued to build great partnerships with Bethel Church and many businesses throughout California. The Calling was also able to be represented in a sponsored trip to Israel and carry its message to many of the nation's leaders. Formation of a massive partnership with Spruce Mountain Ranch launched the motion forward to prepare for the upcoming season.

A Night of Inspiration, Denver, Colorado, October 8, 2015- at Denver University with Rex Crain, Jerry Schlemiel, Voice of the Rockies

"Baby Julie" with The Calling's dear partners in Haiti, i'mMe. This picture captures her "reading" a letter from Calling supporters encouraging her to live out her God-given dreams and casting hope, favor and blessing over her future 2015

2016

Continued planning and creating awareness and finances for the 2020 global conference in Port Au Prince, Haiti. Developed partnership with SONY and The Calling was invited to attend and publicly endorse 2016 movie *Miracles from Heaven* with Golden Globe winner Jennifer Garner at the red carpet premiere. Great partnerships built with City Church LA and Seattle, Warner Brothers, Lakewood Church in Houston Texas, Colorado Christian University, The Ark Museum, Creation Museum, World Vision, and the United States Congress. Spoke at Colorado Christian University Chapel.

2017 – 2020

Speaking at schools and communities around the nation including St. Louis, Colorado and others.

7 Trips to Haiti – Planning and coordinating global conference with the United Nations, Compassion International, El Shalom Church, I'mMe, and so many others

The Calling's Development of Business Plan for all Nations starting in Haiti written by Mellani Day, Dean of CCU Business

Gala and Inspirational Night at Colorado's Governor's Mansion for Haiti and beyond, 'The Power of ONE'

2021 and Beyond

Development of The Calling's Activation Boxes

Development of The Calling's Products

Launch of The Calling's book 'To All the Dreamers'

The Calling's Presence with the National Advisory Board

Development of Dream Dare Cards

Paving the ground work for The Calling's conferences bloom around the world, creating the blueprint of the Imagination Station

The best is yet to come!

SUMMARY OF THE BOOK

This book is for all the Dreamers of the world. This book is for those who wholeheartedly believe that the future belongs to those who dream and yearn to live out God's calling for our lives. Each of us has been given a unique role to fulfill kingdom history for such a time as this. It is now your responsibility to pick the torch you have been given and the relight the flame of your dream once again. Do not let fear hold you back no matter your age, background of culture history. Now is your time and this book was made to let your soar into God's Imagination for you. Be inspired by Chrysandra Brunson's story of starting The Calling to ignite your true calling.

The question is, *'What would do if you knew you could not fail?'*